Thou shalt tell thy son in that day, saying, it is because of that which the **Lord** did for me when I went forth out of **Egypt**.

The Union Haggadah

HOME SERVICE
for the
PASSOVER

EDITED AND PUBLISHED
BY
THE CENTRAL CONFERENCE OF AMERICAN RABBIS
COPYRIGHT 1923

PRINTED IN THE UNITED STATES OF AMERICA

CONTENTS

The Seder — A Foreword.......................... VII
The Union Haggadah.............................. VIII
Rites and Symbols of the Seder.................... XI
Directions for Setting the Table................... XIV
Order of the Service............................. XVI

THE SEDER SERVICE

A. Before the Meal

Lighting of the Festival Lights 3
Kiddush — text and music 4
The Festive Cup, music 14
The Spring-tide of the Year, music................. 17
The Four Questions 18
The Four Sons.................................... 20
The Story of the Oppression....................... 24
Dayenu... 28
The Passover Symbols............................. 34
The Watchnight of the Eternal 38
Psalms CXIII and CXIV — text and music.......... 42
Blessings.. 48

B. After the Meal

To Thee Above, music............................ 54
Grace after the Meal 56
Psalms CXVII and CXVIII: 1–4 — text and music ... 62
Psalms CXVIII: 5–29 — text and music 70
The Final Benediction............................ 78
God of Might, music 80
Addir Hu, music.................................. 81
Our Souls We Raise, music....................... 82
Ki Lo Noeh, music................................ 84
A Madrigal of Numbers — text and music 86
Had Gadyo — text and music 94
Vay'hi Baḥatzi Halay'loh......................... 115
En Kelohenu, music.............................. 118
America, music................................... 120

THE PASSOVER IN HISTORY, LITERATURE AND ART

History of the Passover

A. The Festival of the Shepherds................... 125
B. The Farmer's Spring Festival.................... 127
C. The Feast of Israel's Birth 129

D. The National Celebration
  1. The Passover during the Second Temple......... 130
  2. The Passover Sacrifice........................ 131
E. The Feast of Freedom............................ 133
The Ethical Significance of the Passover............. 134
Moses... 137
Preparation for the Passover
  A. Time of the Feast............................. 139
  B. Matzo-Baking 140
  C. Removing the Leaven......................... 141
  D. Kashering the Utensils........................ 142
Survivals of the Ancient Passover
  A. The Samaritan Passover 143
  B. The Passover as observed by the Falashas......... 145
Passover and Christendom
  A. Passover and Easter........................... 147
  B. Passover and Prejudice 148
  C. Blood Accusation............................. 148
  D. Christian Protests............................ 149
Reform Judaism and Passover....................... 151
  Israel's Journey 152
  Freedom.. 152
  The Season of Joy 153
  The Secret of the Feast.......................... 153
The Haggadah
  A. Growth of its Literature 155
  B. Reform Judaism and the Haggadah.............. 157
  C. Illuminated Haggadahs 159

ILLUSTRATIONS

BOOK PLATE, FRONTISPIECE, BORDERS AND INITIALS
SEDER DISH....................................... X
SEDER EVE 2
THE EXODUS...................................... 41
RELIGIOUS LIBERTY................................ 121
MOSES AND THE TABLES OF THE LAW................. 136

The Seder—A Foreword

Among the ceremonials which nurtured the Jewish idealism of generations, a place of peculiar charm is held by the SEDER, celebrated on the Passover Eve, and repeated on the following night by those who observe the second days of festivals. Literally, the name means THE ORDER of the service. The ritual provided for the service is known as the HAGGADAH, that is, THE NARRATIVE of the Passover. The ceremony grows out of the several injunctions in the Pentateuch for the Israelite TO RELATE to his children the story of the Exodus from Egypt, and to explain to them the meaning of the rites and symbols connected with the celebration of the Passover.

In the Seder are blended, in happy combination, the influences which have contributed so much toward inspiring our people, though scattered throughout the world, with a genuine feeling of kinship. Year after year, the Seder has thrilled them with an appreciation of the glories of their past, imbued them with an heroic power of endurance under the severest trials and persecutions, and quickened within them the enthusiasm of high ideals of freedom.

It has helped to forge "not easily dissoluble links" between the individual and the Jewish people. In his tribute to the poetic beauty of the Seder, Heinrich Heine expressed a sentiment, evidently founded on his personal experience: "It thrills the heart as though one heard the lilt of some sweet lullaby. Even those Jews who have fallen away from the faith of their fathers in the mad pursuit of other joys and other glories are moved to the very depths of their being when by chance they hear again the old Passover melodies once so dear to them."

The Union Haggadah

THE MORAL and spiritual worth of the hallowed institution of the Seder, which has become a vital part of the Jewish consciousness, is priceless. We should suffer an irretrievable loss, were it allowed to pass into neglect. To avert such a danger, has been the anxious thought to which the Union Haggadah owes its origin.

In "carrying on the chain of piety which links the generations to each other", it is necessary frankly to face and honestly to meet the needs of our own day. The old Haggadah, while full of poetic charm, contains passages and sentiments wholly out of harmony with the spirit of the present time. Hence the proper editing of the old material demanded much care and attention on the part of the editors of the first edition of the Union Haggadah. Benefiting by their labors, those entrusted with the task of its revision are able to present a work at once modern in spirit and rich in those traditional elements that lend color to the service.

The Seder service was never purely devotional. Its intensely spiritual tone mingled with bursts of good humor, its serious observations on Jewish life and destiny with comments in a lighter vein, and its lofty poetry with playful ditties for the entertainment of the children. It assumes the form of an historical drama presented at the festal table, with the father and children as leading actors. The children question and the father answers. He explains the nature of the service, preaches, entertains, and prays. In the course of the evening, a complete philosophy of Jewish history is revealed, dealing with Israel's eventful past, with his deliverance from physical and from spiritual bondage, and with his great future world-mission. In its variety, the Haggadah reflects the moods of the Jewish spirit. Rabbinical homily follows dignified narrative, soulful prayers and Psalms mingle with the *Ḥad Gadyo* and the madrigal of numbers, *Eḥod Mi Yode'a*.

The assignment to the child of a prominent part in the Seder service is in consonance with the biblical ordinance: "And thou shalt tell thy son in that day" (Ex. XIII: 8). The visible symbols, the living word of instruction, and the ceremonial acts, are sure to stimulate religious feeling. Parent and child are thus brought into a union of warm religious sympathy, which is all the more indissoluble because strengthened by the ties of natural affection. Their souls are fired with the love of liberty, and their hearts are roused to greater loyalty to Israel and to Israel's God of Freedom.

SEDER DISH

Rites and Symbols of the Seder

THE SEDER service is marked with special concern for the children. A striking contrast is offered between the ceremonies of this service of the Passover Eve and the conduct of the usual meal, so that the child is sure to ask for an explanation, and thus to give the coveted opportunity to tell the story of Israel's deliverance, and to impress the lesson of faith in God, the Defender of right and the Deliverer of the oppressed. These symbols aim to put us in sympathy with our forefathers of the generation of the Exodus; to feel the trials of their embittered life of bondage and the joy of their subsequent triumph of freedom.

WINE. As in all Jewish ceremonials of rejoicing, such as the welcoming of the Sabbath and the festivals, the solemnizing of marriages, and the naming of a child, so at the Seder, wine is used as a token of festivity. Mead, apple-cider, any fruit juice, or especially unfermented raisin wine, is commonly used at the Seder service.

THE FOUR CUPS. Each participant in the service is expected to drink four cups of wine. Even the poorest of the poor who subsist on charity were enjoined to provide themselves with wine for the four cups. This number is determined by the four divine promises of redemption made to Israel in Exodus VI: 6-7: *V'hotzesi, V'hitzalti, V'goalti* and *V'lokaḥti,* that is, bringing out of bondage, deliverance from servitude, redemption from all dependence in Egypt, and selection as "the people of the Lord". The first cup serves for Kiddush as on other holy days and on Sabbath; the second is taken at the conclusion of the first part of the Seder; the third follows the grace after the meal, and the last comes at the end of the second part of the Seder.

THE CUP OF ELIJAH. The fifth promise of God (*V'hevesi*) to bring Israel into Canaan, which follows the four promises of redemption, gave rise to the question of the need of a fifth cup of wine in the Seder. Popular belief left the decision of all mooted questions of law and ritual to the prophet Elijah, the central hero of Jewish legend. The popular mind believed this great champion of righteousness and of pure worship of God to be immortal, and viewed him as the coming forerunner of the Messiah, whose task it will be—among other things—to announce the good tidings of peace and salvation, to effect a union of hearts between parents and their children, to comfort the sorrowing, to raise the dead, and to establish the divine kingdom of righteousness on earth.

The fifth cup, the need of which was left to his decision, came to be known as the Cup of Elijah; and gave rise to the custom of opening the door during the Seder service, that the long expected messenger of the final redemption of mankind from all oppression might enter the home as a most welcome guest. Our fathers were thus helped, in times of darkness and persecution, to keep in mind the Messianic era of freedom, justice, and good-will. Stripped of its legendary form, it is still the hope for the realization of which Israel ever yearns and strives.

MATZO. The unleavened bread or the bread of affliction reminds us of the hardships that our fathers endured in Egypt, and of the haste with which they departed thence. Having no time to bake their bread, they had to rely for food upon sun-baked dough which they carried with them.

WATERCRESS or PARSLEY. Either of these greens is suggestive of the customary oriental relish and is used as a token of gratitude to God for the products of the earth. The purpose of dipping it in salt water or vinegar is to make it palatable.

MOROR. The bitter herb — a piece of horseradish — represents the embittered life of the Israelites in Egypt.

HAROSES. This mixture of apples, blanched almonds, and raisins, finely chopped and flavored with cinnamon and wine, was probably originally a condiment. Owing to its appearance, it came to be regarded as representing the clay with which the Israelites made bricks, or the mortar used in the great structures erected by the bondmen of Egypt.

THE ROASTED SHANK-BONE is an emblem of the Paschal lamb.

THE EGG (roasted) is the symbol of the free-will burnt-offering brought on every day of the feast, during the existence of the Temple in Jerusalem.

APHIKOMON. *Aphikomon* is derived from the Greek, meaning AFTER-MEAL or DESSERT. The origin of this custom must be traced to the Paschal lamb which was eaten on Passover night. It was customary to reserve a small portion of the lamb to be eaten at the close of the meal. When sacrifices had ceased, a piece of the matzo was eaten instead. The *Aphikomon*, hidden early in the Seder, is left to the end of the meal, in order that the children may be kept alert during the entire service. In connection with this, a sort of game of paying forfeits originated. The head of the family good-naturedly takes no note of the spiriting away of the *aphikomon* by the children, who do not surrender it until the master of the house is forced to redeem it by some gift, in order that the meal may be concluded.

Directions for Setting the Table

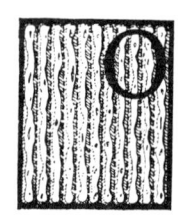

ON the table, in front of the person who conducts the service, place

A large platter containing Seder symbols:

a. Three matzos each of which is covered separately in the folds of a napkin or special cover. Two of them represent the "Leḥem Mishneh — double portion" of the Sabbath and the holy days, and the third the "Leḥem 'Oni — bread of affliction". These are also taken to represent the three religious divisions of Israel: the "Cohen" (priest), "Levi" (associate priest) and "Yisroel" (lay-Israelite).

b. The roasted shank-bone (of a lamb).

c. A roasted egg.

Also a piece of horseradish, a bit of *ḥaroses*, and a spray of parsley.

Besides these, there are placed on the table for the company:

1. A plate of bitter herbs (horseradish), cut into small pieces.

2. A dish of *ḥaroses*.

3. Parsley or watercress.

4. A dish of salt water.

xiv

5. A cup of wine is placed at each plate, and a large brimming goblet in the center of the table for the prophet Elijah.

The meal served during the Seder follows the form of a banquet of olden times. Hence the reference, in the Hebrew texts of the Four Questions, to the custom of reclining on the left side—a position assumed by free men. Preserving this custom, many households still provide a large cushioned armchair for the person conducting the Seder.

The table is usually spread with the best of the family's china and silverware, and adorned with flowers, in keeping with the festive spirit.

Order of the Service

1. Recite the Kiddush (Sanctification of the festival). — קַדֵּשׁ
2. Partake of parsley dipped in salt water. — כַּרְפַּס
3. Break the middle Matzo, and hide one part to be eaten at the end of the meal as the Aphikomon. — יַחַץ
4. Tell the story of Israel's deliverance from Egyptian bondage. — מַגִּיד
5. Recite the blessing before the meal, including the special blessing over Matzo. — מוֹצִיא, מַצָּה
6. Combine Matzo, Moror and Haroses and eat them together. — כּוֹרֵךְ, מָרוֹר
7. Partake of the festival meal. — שֻׁלְחָן עוֹרֵךְ
8. Conclude the meal by eating the Aphikomon. — צָפוּן
9. Say grace after the meal. — בָּרֵךְ
10. Recite the remainder of the Hallel· — הַלֵּל
11. End with a prayer for the acceptance of the service. — נִרְצָה

The Seder Service

A. Before the Meal

SEDER EVE

1. קַדֵּשׁ

Lighting the Festival Lights

To symbolize the joy which the festival brings into the Jewish home, the mistress kindles the lights and recites the following blessing:

בָּרוּךְ אַתָּה יְיָ אֱלֹהֵינוּ מֶלֶךְ הָעוֹלָם אֲשֶׁר קִדְּשָׁנוּ בְּמִצְוֹתָיו וְצִוָּנוּ לְהַדְלִיק נֵר שֶׁל־(שַׁבָּת וְשֶׁל־) יוֹם טוֹב.

ORUCH ATTO ADONOI ELOHENU MELECH HO'OLOM ASHER KIDD'SHONU B'-MITZVOSOV V'TZIVONU L'HADLIK NER SHEL (*on Sabbath add:* SHABBOS V'SHEL) YOM TOV.

בָּרוּךְ אַתָּה יְיָ אֱלֹהֵינוּ מֶלֶךְ הָעוֹלָם. שֶׁהֶחֱיָנוּ וְקִיְּמָנוּ וְהִגִּיעָנוּ לַזְּמַן הַזֶּה:

BORUCH ATTO ADONOI ELOHENU MELECH HO'OLOM SHEHEHEYONU V'KIY'MONU V'HIGIONU LAZMAN HAZZEH.

Praised art Thou, O Lord our God, King of the universe, who hast sanctified us by Thy commandments, and hast commanded us to kindle the (*on Sabbath add:* Sabbath and) festival lights.

Praised art Thou, O Lord our God, King of the universe, who hast kept us alive and sustained us and brought us to this season.

May our home be consecrated, O God, by the light of Thy countenance, shining upon us in blessing, and bringing us peace!

Company: Amen.

Kiddush

On Sabbath eve begin here.

The master of the house lifts up the wine-cup and says:

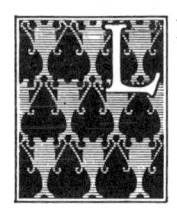

LET US praise God and thank Him for all the blessings of the week that is gone; for life, health and strength; for home, love and friendship; for the discipline of our trials and temptations; for the happiness of our success and prosperity. Thou hast ennobled us, O God, by the blessings of work, and in love and grace sanctified us by the blessings of rest, through the commandment, "Six days shalt thou labor and do all thy work, but the seventh day is a Sabbath unto the Lord thy God".

On weeks days begin here.

With song and praise, and with the symbols of our feast, let us renew the memories of our past.

Praised art Thou, O Lord our God, King of the universe, who hast chosen us from all peoples and exalted and sanctified us with Thy commandments. In love hast Thou given us, O Lord our God, solemn days of joy and festive seasons of gladness, even this day of the Feast of Unleavened Bread, a holy convocation unto us, a memorial of the departure from Egypt. Thou hast chosen us for Thy service and

קִדּוּשׁ

On Sabbath eve begin here.

וֹם הַשִּׁשִּׁי: וַיְכֻלּוּ הַשָּׁמַיִם וְהָאָרֶץ וְכָל־צְבָאָם: וַיְכַל אֱלֹהִים בַּיּוֹם הַשְּׁבִיעִי מְלַאכְתּוֹ אֲשֶׁר עָשָׂה וַיִּשְׁבֹּת בַּיּוֹם הַשְּׁבִיעִי מִכָּל־מְלַאכְתּוֹ אֲשֶׁר עָשָׂה: וַיְבָרֶךְ אֱלֹהִים אֶת־יוֹם הַשְּׁבִיעִי וַיְקַדֵּשׁ אֹתוֹ כִּי בוֹ שָׁבַת מִכָּל־מְלַאכְתּוֹ אֲשֶׁר־בָּרָא אֱלֹהִים לַעֲשׂוֹת:

On week days begin here.

*) בָּרוּךְ אַתָּה יְיָ אֱלֹהֵינוּ מֶלֶךְ הָעוֹלָם. אֲשֶׁר בָּחַר בָּנוּ מִכָּל־עָם. וְרוֹמְמָנוּ מִכָּל־לָשׁוֹן. וְקִדְּשָׁנוּ בְּמִצְוֹתָיו. וַתִּתֶּן־לָנוּ יְיָ אֱלֹהֵינוּ בְּאַהֲבָה. וְשַׁבָּתוֹת לִמְנוּחָה. וּמוֹעֲדִים לְשִׂמְחָה. חַגִּים וּזְמַנִּים לְשָׂשׂוֹן אֶת־יוֹם וְהַשַּׁבָּת הַזֶּה. וְאֶת־יוֹם חַג הַמַּצּוֹת הַזֶּה. זְמַן חֵרוּתֵנוּ מִקְרָא קֹדֶשׁ. זֵכֶר לִיצִיאַת מִצְרָיִם: כִּי בָנוּ בָחַרְתָּ. וְאוֹתָנוּ קִדַּשְׁתָּ מִכָּל־הָעַמִּים. וְשַׁבָּתוֹ

*) The Kiddush may be chanted to the music given on the following pages.

hast made us sharers in the blessings of Thy holy festivals. Blessed art Thou, O Lord, who sanctifiest Israel and the festive seasons.

All read in unison:

BORUCH ATTO ADONOI ELOHENU MELECH HO'OLOM BORE P'RI HAGGOFEN.

Praised art Thou, O Lord our God, Ruler of the world, who hast created the fruit of the vine.

Drink the first cup of wine.

וּמוֹעֲדֵי קָדְשֶׁךָ. וּבְאַהֲבָה וּבְרָצוֹן. בְּשִׂמְחָה וּבְשָׂשׂוֹן הִנְחַלְתָּנוּ: בָּרוּךְ אַתָּה יְיָ. מְקַדֵּשׁ וְהַשַּׁבָּת חְיִשְׂרָאֵל וְהַזְּמַנִּים:

All read in unison:

בָּרוּךְ אַתָּה יְיָ אֱלֹהֵינוּ מֶלֶךְ הָעוֹלָם בּוֹרֵא פְּרִי הַגָּפֶן:

Drink the first cup of wine.

Kiddush

SOLO. Recit.
parlando

Bo - ruch at - toh a - do - noi

CHORUS — bo - ruch hu u - vo - ruch sh' - mo

SOLO — e - lo - he - nu melech ho - o - lom............ bo - re p'-

ri........ hag-gofen O-men. Bo-ruch attoh a-do-noi bo-ruch hu u-vo-ruch sh'-mo e-lo-he-nu me-lech ho-o-lom a-sher bo-ḥar bo-nu mik-kol

om........ v'-ro-m'-mo-nu mik-kol lo-
shon v'kid-d'-sho-nu b'-mitz-vo-sov vat-ti-ten
lo-nu a-do-noi e-lo-he-nu b'-a-ha-voh

(shab-bos-sos lim'nu-ḥo u-)mo-a-dim l'-sim-ḥoh ḥag-gim uz-ma-
nim l'-so - son es yom ḥag ham - ma - tzos haz - zeh
z' man ḥe - ru - se - nu mik-ro ko - desh

ze-cher li - tzi - as mitz - ro-yim ki vo - nu vo-har - -
to v - o- so - nu kid - dash - to mi - kol ho-am-mim umo-a-
de kod - she- cho b'-sim - ho u - v'so - son........

CHOR.
..... hin-hal-to - nu bo - ruch at-toh a-do-noi! Bo -
SOLO
ruch hu u - vo - ruch sh' - mo m' - kad -
CHOR.
desh yis-ro-el v'- haz - - - z'- ma-nim O-men.

The Festive Cup

SOLO. *Maestoso*

The fes - tive wine cup let us raise, To - geth - er let us, let us sing, With
He saved our sires from ev -'ry foe, By Him all slaves, all slaves were freed; Our

hearts o'er-flow-ing let us praise, Our
help is He in joy and woe, Our

CHORUS

God our heav'nly King; With hearts o'er-flow-ing
stay in time of need; Our help is He in

let us praise, Our God our heav'nly King.
joy and woe, Our stay in time of need.

2. כַּרְפַּס

Some parsley, lettuce or watercress is distributed to all present who dip it in salt water or in vinegar, and before partaking of it say in unison:

בָּרוּךְ אַתָּה יְיָ אֱלֹהֵינוּ מֶלֶךְ הָעוֹלָם בּוֹרֵא פְּרִי הָאֲדָמָה:

BORUCH ATTO ADONOI ELOHENU MELECH HO'OLOM BORE P'RI HO'ADOMO.

Praised art Thou, O Lord our God, King of the universe, Creator of the fruit of the earth.

3. יַחַץ

The leader breaks the middle Matzo, leaving one half on the Seder-dish, and hiding the other half as the Aphikomon to be eaten at the end of the meal.

The Spring-tide of the Year

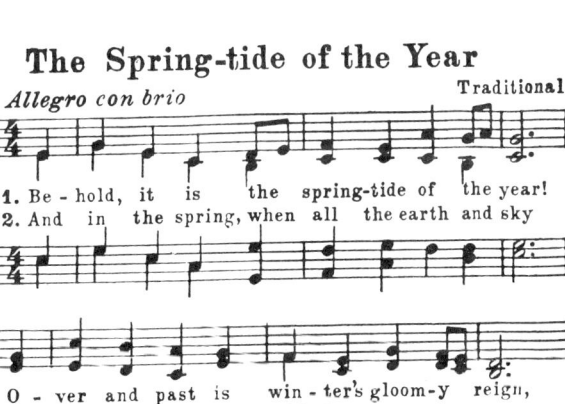

Allegro con brio
Traditional

1. Be - hold, it is the spring-tide of the year!
   O - ver and past is win - ter's gloom-y reign,
   The hap - py time of sing - ing birds is near,
   And clad in bud and bloom are hill and plain.

2. And in the spring, when all the earth and sky
   Re - joice to - geth - er, still from age to age
   Rings out the sol - emn chant of days gone by,
   Pro - claim-ing Is - rael's sa - cred her - i - tage.

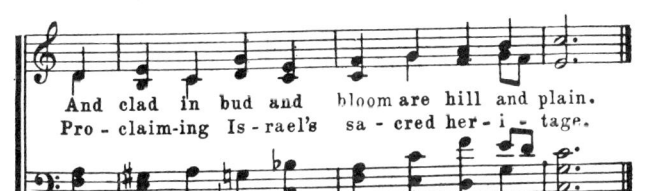

3. For as from out the house of bondage went
   The host of Israel, in their midst they bore
   The heritage of law and freedom, blent
   In holy unity for evermore.

4. And still from rising unto setting sun
   Shall this our heritage and watchword be:
   "The Lord our God, the Lord our God is One;
   His law alone it is that makes us free!"

4. מַגִּיד

The leader lifts up the Matzos and says:

Lo! This is the bread of affliction which our fathers ate in the land of Egypt. Let all who are hungry come and eat. Let all who are in want come and celebrate the Passover with us. May it be God's will to redeem us from all trouble and from all servitude. Next year at this season, may the whole house of Israel be free!

The leader replaces the dish upon the table.

The Four Questions

The youngest person at the table asks:

WHY IS this night different from all other nights? On all other nights, we eat either leavened or unleavened bread. Why, on this night, do we eat only unleavened bread?

2. On all other nights, we eat all kinds of herbs. Why, on this night, do we eat especially bitter herbs?

3. On all other nights, we do not dip herbs in any condiment. Why, on this night, do we dip them in salt water and ḥaroses?

4. On all other nights, we eat without special festivities. Why, on this night, do we hold this Seder service?

4. מַגִּיד

הָא לַחְמָא עַנְיָא דִי אֲכָלוּ אֲבָהֳתָנָא בְּאַרְעָא דְמִצְרָיִם. כָּל דִּכְפִין יֵיתֵי וְיֵכֹל. כָּל־דִּצְרִיךְ יֵיתֵי וְיִפְסַח. יְהֵא רַעֲוָא קֳדָם מָרָנָא דִי בִשְׁמַיָּא. דִי יִפְרֹק יָתָנָא מִדְּכָל־עָקָא. וְיֶהֱוֵא כָּל־בֵּית יִשְׂרָאֵל. בְּשַׁתָּא דְאָתְיָא בְּנֵי חוֹרִין:

The youngest person asks:

ה נִשְׁתַּנָּה הַלַּיְלָה הַזֶּה מִכָּל הַלֵּילוֹת. שֶׁבְּכָל הַלֵּילוֹת אָנוּ אוֹכְלִין חָמֵץ וּמַצָּה. הַלַּיְלָה הַזֶּה כֻּלּוֹ מַצָּה: שֶׁבְּכָל הַלֵּילוֹת אָנוּ אוֹכְלִין שְׁאָר יְרָקוֹת. הַלַּיְלָה הַזֶּה מָרוֹר: שֶׁבְּכָל הַלֵּילוֹת אֵין אָנוּ מַטְבִּילִין אֲפִילוּ פַּעַם אֶחָת. הַלַּיְלָה הַזֶּה שְׁתֵּי פְעָמִים: שֶׁבְּכָל הַלֵּילוֹת אָנוּ אוֹכְלִין בֵּין יוֹשְׁבִין וּבֵין מְסֻבִּין. הַלַּיְלָה הַזֶּה כֻּלָּנוּ מְסֻבִּין:

The leader answers:

We celebrate to-night because we were Pharaoh's bondmen in Egypt, and the Lord our God delivered us with a mighty hand. Had not the Holy One, blessed be He, redeemed our fathers from Egypt, we, our children, and our children's children would have remained slaves. Therefore even if all of us were wise and well-versed in the Torah, it would still be our duty from year to year, to tell the story of the deliverance from Egypt. Indeed to dwell at length on it, is accounted praiseworthy.

The Four Sons

BY A fitting answer to the questions of each of the four types of the sons of Israel, does the Torah explain the meaning of this night's celebration.

The wise son eager to learn asks earnestly: "What mean the testimonies and the statutes and the ordinances, which the Lord our God hath commanded us?" To him thou shalt say: "This service is held in order to worship the Lord our God, that it may be well with us all the days of our life".

The wicked son inquires in a mocking spirit: "What mean YE by this service?" As he says YE and not WE, he excludes himself from the household of Israel. Therefore thou shouldst turn on him and say: "It is because of that which the Lord did for ME when I came forth out of Egypt". For ME and not for HIM, for had he been there, he would not have been found worthy of being redeemed.

The leader answers:

עֲבָדִים הָיִינוּ לְפַרְעֹה בְּמִצְרָיִם. וַיּוֹצִיאֵנוּ יְיָ אֱלֹהֵינוּ מִשָּׁם בְּיָד חֲזָקָה וּבִזְרוֹעַ נְטוּיָה. וְאִלּוּ לֹא הוֹצִיא הַקָּדוֹשׁ בָּרוּךְ הוּא אֶת־אֲבוֹתֵינוּ מִמִּצְרָיִם. הֲרֵי אָנוּ וּבָנֵינוּ וּבְנֵי בָנֵינוּ מְשֻׁעְבָּדִים הָיִינוּ לְפַרְעֹה בְּמִצְרָיִם. וַאֲפִילוּ כֻּלָּנוּ חֲכָמִים. כֻּלָּנוּ נְבוֹנִים. כֻּלָּנוּ זְקֵנִים. כֻּלָּנוּ יוֹדְעִים אֶת־הַתּוֹרָה. מִצְוָה עָלֵינוּ לְסַפֵּר בִּיצִיאַת מִצְרָיִם. וְכָל הַמַּרְבֶּה לְסַפֵּר בִּיצִיאַת מִצְרַיִם הֲרֵי זֶה מְשֻׁבָּח:

כְּנֶגֶד אַרְבָּעָה בָנִים דִּבְּרָה תוֹרָה. אֶחָד חָכָם. וְאֶחָד רָשָׁע. וְאֶחָד תָּם. וְאֶחָד שֶׁאֵינוֹ יוֹדֵעַ לִשְׁאֹל:

חָכָם מָה הוּא אוֹמֵר. מָה הָעֵדֹת וְהַחֻקִּים וְהַמִּשְׁפָּטִים אֲשֶׁר צִוָּה יְיָ אֱלֹהֵינוּ אֶתְכֶם: וְאַף אַתָּה אֱמָר־לוֹ. לְיִרְאָה אֶת־יְיָ אֱלֹהֵינוּ. לְטוֹב לָנוּ כָּל־הַיָּמִים:

רָשָׁע מָה הוּא אוֹמֵר. מָה הָעֲבֹדָה הַזֹּאת לָכֶם. לָכֶם וְלֹא לוֹ. וּלְפִי שֶׁהוֹצִיא אֶת עַצְמוֹ מִן הַכְּלָל כָּפַר בְּעִקָּר. וְאַף אַתָּה הַקְהֵה אֶת־שִׁנָּיו וֶאֱמוֹר לוֹ בַּעֲבוּר זֶה עָשָׂה יְיָ לִי בְּצֵאתִי מִמִּצְרָיִם. לִי וְלֹא לָךְ. אִלּוּ הָיִיתָ שָׁם. לֹא הָיִיתָ נִגְאָל:

The simple son indifferently asks: "What is this?" To him thou shalt say: "By strength of hand the Lord brought us out of Egypt, out of the house of bondage".

And for the son who is unable to inquire, thou shalt explain the whole story of the Passover; as it is said: "And thou shalt tell thy son in that day, saying 'It is because of that which the Lord did for me when I came forth out of Egypt'".

תָּם מָה הוּא אוֹמֵר. מַה־זֹּאת. וְאָמַרְתָּ אֵלָיו.
בְּחֹזֶק יָד הוֹצִיאָנוּ יְיָ מִמִּצְרַיִם מִבֵּית עֲבָדִים:
וְשֶׁאֵינוֹ יוֹדֵעַ לִשְׁאוֹל. אַתְּ פְּתַח לוֹ. שֶׁנֶּאֱמַר
וְהִגַּדְתָּ לְבִנְךָ בַּיּוֹם הַהוּא לֵאמֹר. בַּעֲבוּר זֶה עָשָׂה
יְיָ לִי בְּצֵאתִי מִמִּצְרָיִם:

The Story of the Oppression

IT IS well for all of us whether young or old to consider how God's help has been our unfailing stay and support through ages of trial and persecution. Ever since He called our father Abraham from the bondage of idolatry to His service of truth, He has been our Guardian; for not in one country alone nor in one age have violent men risen up against us, but in every generation and in every land, tyrants have sought to destroy us; and the Holy One, blessed be He, has delivered us from their hands.

The Torah tells us that when Jacob our father was a homeless wanderer, he went down into Egypt, and sojourned there, few in number. All the souls of his household were threescore and ten. And Joseph was already in Egypt; he was the governor over the land. And Joseph placed his father and his brethren, and gave them a possession, as Pharaoh had commanded. And Israel dwelt in the land of Goshen; and they got them possessions therein, and were fruitful, and multiplied exceedingly.

And Joseph died, and all his brethren, and all that generation. Now there arose a new king over Egypt, who knew not Joseph. And he said unto his people: 'Behold, the people of the children of Israel are too many and too mighty for us; come, let us deal wisely

הִיא שֶׁעָמְדָה לַאֲבוֹתֵינוּ וְלָנוּ. שֶׁלֹּא אֶחָד בִּלְבָד עָמַד עָלֵינוּ לְכַלּוֹתֵינוּ. אֶלָּא שֶׁבְּכָל דּוֹר וָדוֹר עוֹמְדִים עָלֵינוּ לְכַלּוֹתֵינוּ. וְהַקָּדוֹשׁ בָּרוּךְ הוּא מַצִּילֵנוּ מִיָּדָם:

אֲרַמִּי אֹבֵד אָבִי וַיֵּרֶד מִצְרַיְמָה וַיָּגָר שָׁם בִּמְתֵי מְעָט. כָּל־הַנֶּפֶשׁ לְבֵית־יַעֲקֹב הַבָּאָה מִצְרַיְמָה שִׁבְעִים. וְיוֹסֵף הָיָה בְמִצְרָיִם. הוּא הַשַּׁלִּיט עַל הָאָרֶץ. וַיּוֹשֵׁב יוֹסֵף אֶת־אָבִיו וְאֶת־אֶחָיו וַיִּתֵּן לָהֶם אֲחֻזָּה כַּאֲשֶׁר צִוָּה פַרְעֹה. וַיֵּשֶׁב יִשְׂרָאֵל בְּאֶרֶץ גֹּשֶׁן. וַיְהִי־שָׁם לְגוֹי גָּדוֹל עָצוּם וָרָב.

וַיָּקָם מֶלֶךְ־חָדָשׁ עַל־מִצְרָיִם אֲשֶׁר לֹא־יָדַע אֶת־יוֹסֵף. וַיֹּאמֶר אֶל־עַמּוֹ הִנֵּה עַם בְּנֵי יִשְׂרָאֵל רַב וְעָצוּם מִמֶּנּוּ. הָבָה נִתְחַכְּמָה לוֹ פֶּן־יִרְבֶּה וְהָיָה

with them, lest they multiply, and it come to pass, that when there befalleth us any war, they also join themselves unto our enemies, and fight against us, and get them up out of the land'. Therefore they set over them taskmasters to afflict them with burdens. And they built for Pharaoh store-cities, Pithom and Raamses. But the more the Egyptians afflicted them, the more the Israelites multiplied and the more they spread abroad.

And the Egyptians dealt ill with us, and afflicted us, and laid upon us cruel bondage. And we cried unto the Lord, the God of our fathers, and the Lord heard our voice and saw our affliction and our toil and our oppression. And the Lord brought us forth out of Egypt, with a mighty hand and with an outstretched arm and with great terror and with signs and with wonders. He sent before us Moses and Aaron and Miriam. And He brought forth His people with joy, His chosen ones with singing. And He guided them in the wilderness, as a shepherd his flock.

Therefore He commanded us to observe the Passover in its season, from year to year, that His law shall be in our mouths, and that we shall declare His might unto our children, His salvation to all generations.

All read in unison:

Who is like unto Thee, O Lord, among the mighty?
  Who is like unto Thee, glorious in holiness,
  Fearful in praises, doing wonders?
The Lord shall reign for ever and ever.

כִּי־תִקְרֶאנָה מִלְחָמָה וְנוֹסַף גַּם־הוּא עַל־שֹׂנְאֵינוּ וְנִלְחַם־בָּנוּ וְעָלָה מִן־הָאָרֶץ. וַיָּשִׂימוּ עָלָיו שָׂרֵי מִסִּים לְמַעַן עַנֹּתוֹ בְּסִבְלֹתָם וַיִּבֶן עָרֵי מִסְכְּנוֹת לְפַרְעֹה אֶת־פִּתֹם וְאֶת־רַעַמְסֵס. וְכַאֲשֶׁר יְעַנּוּ אֹתוֹ כֵּן יִרְבֶּה וְכֵן יִפְרֹץ.

וַיָּרֵעוּ אֹתָנוּ הַמִּצְרִים וַיְעַנּוּנוּ וַיִּתְּנוּ עָלֵינוּ עֲבֹדָה קָשָׁה. וַנִּצְעַק אֶל־יְיָ אֱלֹהֵי אֲבוֹתֵינוּ וַיִּשְׁמַע יְיָ אֶת־קֹלֵנוּ וַיַּרְא אֶת־עָנְיֵנוּ וְאֶת־עֲמָלֵנוּ וְאֶת־לַחֲצֵנוּ. וַיּוֹצִיאֵנוּ יְיָ מִמִּצְרַיִם בְּיָד חֲזָקָה וּבִזְרֹעַ נְטוּיָה וּבְמֹרָא גָּדֹל וּבְאֹתוֹת וּבְמֹפְתִים. וַיִּשְׁלַח לְפָנֵינוּ אֶת מֹשֶׁה אַהֲרֹן וּמִרְיָם. וַיּוֹצֵא עַמּוֹ בְּשָׂשׂוֹן בְּרִנָּה אֶת־בְּחִירָיו. וַיַּנְהֲגֵם בַּמִּדְבָּר כְּרֹעֶה עֶדְרוֹ.

וַיְצַוֵּנוּ לַעֲשׂוֹת אֶת־הַפֶּסַח לְזִכָּרוֹן בְּמוֹעֲדוֹ מִיָּמִים יָמִימָה. לְמַעַן תִּהְיֶה תּוֹרָתוֹ בְּפִינוּ וּלְמַעַן נַגִּיד גְּבוּרָתוֹ לְבָנֵינוּ. יְשׁוּעָתוֹ לְדוֹר וָדוֹר.

All read in unison:

מִי־כָמֹכָה בָּאֵלִם יְיָ מִי כָּמֹכָה נֶאְדָּר בַּקֹּדֶשׁ נוֹרָא תְהִלֹּת עֹשֵׂה־פֶלֶא. יְיָ יִמְלֹךְ לְעֹלָם וָעֶד.

27

Dayenu

The company repeats the refrain "Dayenu" which is equivalent to "It would have satisfied us".

How manifold are the favors which God has conferred upon us!

HAD HE brought us out of Egypt, and not divided the sea for us, Dayenu!

HAD HE divided the sea, and not permitted us to cross on dry land, Dayenu!

HAD HE permitted us to cross the sea on dry land, and not sustained us for forty years in the desert, Dayenu!

HAD HE sustained us for forty years in the desert, and not fed us with manna,

Dayenu!

כַּמָּה מַעֲלוֹת טוֹבוֹת לַמָּקוֹם עָלֵינוּ:

אִלוּ הוֹצִיאָנוּ מִמִּצְרַיִם.
וְלֹא קָרַע לָנוּ אֶת הַיָּם.　　דַּיֵּנוּ:

אִלוּ קָרַע לָנוּ אֶת הַיָּם.
וְלֹא הֶעֱבִירָנוּ בְתוֹכוֹ בֶּחָרָבָה　　דַּיֵּנוּ:

אִלוּ הֶעֱבִירָנוּ בְתוֹכוֹ בֶּחָרָבָה.
וְלֹא סִפֵּק צָרְכֵּנוּ בַּמִּדְבָּר אַרְבָּעִים שָׁנָה　　דַּיֵּנוּ:

אִלוּ סִפֵּק צָרְכֵּנוּ בַּמִּדְבָּר אַרְבָּעִים שָׁנָה
וְלֹא הֶאֱכִילָנוּ אֶת־הַמָּן　　דַּיֵּנוּ:

HAD HE fed us with manna, and not ordained the Sabbath, Dayenu!

HAD HE ordained the Sabbath, and not brought us to Mount Sinai, Dayenu!

HAD HE brought us to Mount Sinai, and not given us the Torah, Dayenu!

HAD HE given us the Torah, and not led us into the Land of Israel, Dayenu!

HAD HE led us into the Land of Israel, and not built for us the Temple, Dayenu!

HAD HE built for us the Temple, and not sent us prophets of truth, Dayenu!

HAD HE sent us prophets of truth, and not made us a holy people, Dayenu!

לוּ הֶאֱכִילָנוּ אֶת־הַמָּן.
וְלֹא נָתַן לָנוּ אֶת־הַשַּׁבָּת. דַּיֵּנוּ:

לוּ נָתַן לָנוּ אֶת־הַשַּׁבָּת.
וְלֹא קֵרְבָנוּ לִפְנֵי הַר סִינַי דַּיֵּנוּ:

לוּ קֵרְבָנוּ לִפְנֵי הַר סִינַי.
וְלֹא נָתַן לָנוּ אֶת־הַתּוֹרָה דַּיֵּנוּ:

לוּ נָתַן לָנוּ אֶת־הַתּוֹרָה.
וְלֹא הִכְנִיסָנוּ לְאֶרֶץ יִשְׂרָאֵל דַּיֵּנוּ:

לוּ הִכְנִיסָנוּ לְאֶרֶץ יִשְׂרָאֵל.
וְלֹא בָנָה לָנוּ אֶת־בֵּית הַבְּחִירָה דַּיֵּנוּ:

לוּ בָנָה לָנוּ אֶת־בֵּית הַבְּחִירָה
וְלֹא שָׁלַח אֵלֵינוּ נְבִיאֵי הָאֱמֶת. דַּיֵּנוּ:

לוּ שָׁלַח אֵלֵינוּ נְבִיאֵי הָאֱמֶת.
וְלֹא שָׂמָנוּ לְעַם קָדוֹשׁ. דַּיֵּנוּ:

All read in unison:

How much more then are we to be grateful unto the Lord for the manifold favors which He has bestowed upon us! He brought us out of Egypt, divided the Red Sea for us, permitted us to cross on dry land, sustained us for forty years in the desert, fed us with manna, ordained the Sabbath, brought us to Mount Sinai, gave us the Torah, led us into the Land of Israel, built for us the Temple, sent unto us prophets of truth, and made us a holy people to perfect the world under the kingdom of the Almighty, in truth and in righteousness.

All read in unison:

עַל אַחַת כַּמָּה וְכַמָּה טוֹבָה כְפוּלָה וּמְכֻפֶּלֶת לַמָּקוֹם עָלֵינוּ. שֶׁהוֹצִיאָנוּ מִמִּצְרַיִם. וְקָרַע לָנוּ אֶת הַיָּם. וְהֶעֱבִירָנוּ בְּתוֹכוֹ בֶּחָרָבָה. וְסִפֵּק צָרְכֵּנוּ בַּמִּדְבָּר אַרְבָּעִים שָׁנָה. וְהֶאֱכִילָנוּ אֶת־הַמָּן. וְנָתַן לָנוּ אֶת־הַשַּׁבָּת. וְקֵרְבָנוּ לִפְנֵי הַר סִינַי. וְנָתַן לָנוּ אֶת־הַתּוֹרָה. וְהִכְנִיסָנוּ לְאֶרֶץ יִשְׂרָאֵל. וּבָנָה לָנוּ אֶת־בֵּית הַבְּחִירָה. וְשָׁלַח אֵלֵינוּ נְבִיאֵי הָאֱמֶת. וְשָׂמָנוּ לְעַם קָדוֹשׁ לְתַקֵּן עוֹלָם בְּמַלְכוּת שַׁדַּי בֶּאֱמֶת וּבִצְדָקָה.

The Passover Symbols

Should enemies again assail us, the remembrance of the exodus of our fathers from Egypt will never fail to inspire us with new courage, and the symbols of this festival will help to strengthen our faith in God, who redeems the oppressed.

Therefore, Rabban Gamaliel, a noted sage, declared: "Whoever does not well consider the meaning of these three symbols: Pesaḥ, Matzo and Moror, has not truly celebrated this Festival".

PESAḤ

One of the company asks:

WHAT is the meaning of Pesaḥ?

The leader lifts up the roasted shank-bone and answers:

Pesaḥ means the PASCHAL LAMB, and is symbolized by this shank-bone. It was eaten by our fathers while the Temple was in existence, as a memorial of God's favors, as it is said: "It is the sacrifice of the Lord's PASSOVER, for that He PASSED OVER the houses of the children of Israel in Egypt, when He smote the Egyptians and delivered our houses". As God in the ancient "Watch-Night" passed over and spared the houses of Israel, so did He save us in all kinds of distress, and so may He always shield the afflicted, and for ever remove every trace of bondage from among the children of man.

רַבָּן גַּמְלִיאֵל הָיָה אוֹמֵר. כָּל־שֶׁלֹּא אָמַר שְׁלֹשָׁה דְבָרִים אֵלּוּ בַּפֶּסַח לֹא יָצָא יְדֵי חוֹבָתוֹ. וְאֵלּוּ הֵן. פֶּסַח. מַצָּה. וּמָרוֹר:

One of the company asks:

פֶּסַח שֶׁהָיוּ אֲבוֹתֵינוּ אֹכְלִין בִּזְמַן שֶׁבֵּית הַמִּקְדָּשׁ הָיָה קַיָּם עַל־שׁוּם מָה.

The leader lifts up the roasted shank-bone and answers:

פֶּסַח שֶׁהָיוּ אֲבוֹתֵינוּ אֹכְלִין בִּזְמַן שֶׁבֵּית הַמִּקְדָּשׁ הָיָה קַיָּם עַל־שׁוּם שֶׁפֶּסַח הַקָּדוֹשׁ בָּרוּךְ הוּא עַל בָּתֵּי אֲבוֹתֵינוּ בְּמִצְרָיִם. שֶׁנֶּאֱמַר. וַאֲמַרְתֶּם זֶבַח פֶּסַח הוּא לַיָי אֲשֶׁר פָּסַח עַל־בָּתֵּי בְנֵי יִשְׂרָאֵל בְּמִצְרָיִם. וּכְשֵׁם שֶׁגָּאַל הַקָּדוֹשׁ בָּרוּךְ הוּא אֶת־אֲבוֹתֵינוּ מִמִּצְרָיִם בְּחִפָּזוֹן. כֵּן יָגֵן עָלֵינוּ בְּכָל־יוֹם תָּמִיד. גָּנוֹן וְהַצִּיל פָּסוֹחַ וְהַמְלִיט:

MATZO

One of the company asks:

What is the meaning of Matzo?

The leader lifts up the Matzo and answers:

Matzo, called THE BREAD OF AFFLICTION, was the hasty provision that our fathers made for their journey, as it is said: "And they baked unleavened cakes of the dough which they brought out of Egypt. There was not sufficient time to leaven it, for they were driven out of Egypt and could not tarry, neither had they prepared for themselves any provisions." The bread which of necessity they baked unleavened, thus became a symbol of divine help.

MOROR

One of the company asks:

And what is the meaning of MOROR?

The leader lifts up the bitter herbs and answers:

Moror means BITTER HERB. We eat it in order to recall that the lives of our ancestors were embittered by the Egyptians, as we read: 'And they made their lives bitter with hard labor in mortar and bricks and in all manner of field labor. Whatever task was imposed upon them, was executed with the utmost rigor." As we eat it in the midst of the festivities of this night, we rejoice in the heroic spirit which trials developed in our people. Instead of becoming embittered by them, they were sustained and strengthened.

One of the company asks:

מַצָּה זוּ שֶׁאָנוּ אוֹכְלִין עַל־שׁוּם מָה.

The leader lifts up the Matzo and answers:

מַצָּה זוּ שֶׁאָנוּ אוֹכְלִין עַל שֵׁם שֶׁלֹּא הִסְפִּיק בְּצֵקָם שֶׁל אֲבוֹתֵינוּ לְהַחֲמִיץ. עַד שֶׁנִּגְלָה עֲלֵיהֶם מֶלֶךְ מַלְכֵי הַמְּלָכִים הַקָּדוֹשׁ בָּרוּךְ הוּא וּגְאָלָם. שֶׁנֶּאֱמַר. וַיֹּאפוּ־אֶת־הַבָּצֵק אֲשֶׁר הוֹצִיאוּ מִמִּצְרַיִם עֻגֹת מַצּוֹת כִּי לֹא חָמֵץ כִּי־גֹרְשׁוּ מִמִּצְרַיִם וְלֹא יָכְלוּ לְהִתְמַהְמֵהַּ וְגַם־צֵדָה לֹא־עָשׂוּ לָהֶם:

One of the company asks:

מָרוֹר זֶה שֶׁאָנוּ אוֹכְלִין עַל־שׁוּם מָה.

The leader lifts up the Moror and answers:

מָרוֹר זֶה שֶׁאָנוּ אוֹכְלִין עַל־שׁוּם שֶׁמֵּרְרוּ הַמִּצְרִים אֶת חַיֵּי אֲבוֹתֵינוּ בְּמִצְרָיִם. שֶׁנֶּאֱמַר. וַיְמָרֲרוּ אֶת חַיֵּיהֶם בַּעֲבֹדָה קָשָׁה בְּחֹמֶר וּבִלְבֵנִים וּבְכָל עֲבֹדָה בַּשָּׂדֶה אֵת כָּל־עֲבֹדָתָם אֲשֶׁר־עָבְדוּ בָהֶם בְּפָרֶךְ:

The Watch-night of the Eternal

IN EVERY generation, each Jew should regard himself as though he too were brought out of Egypt. Not our fathers alone, but us also, did the Holy One redeem; for not alone in Egypt but in many other lands, have we groaned under the burden of affliction and suffered as victims of malice, ignorance and fanaticism. This very night which we, a happy generation, celebrate so calmly and safely and joyfully in our habitations was often turned into a night of anxiety and of suffering for our people in former times. Cruel mobs were ready to rush upon them and to destroy their homes and the fruit of their labors. But undauntedly they clung to their faith in the ultimate triumph of right and of freedom. Champions of God, they marched from one Egypt into another—driven in haste, their property a prey to the rapacious foe, with their bundles on their shoulders, and God in their hearts.

Because God, "the Guardian of Israel, who sleepeth not nor slumbereth" revealed Himself on that WATCH-NIGHT IN EGYPT and in all dark periods of our past, as the Redeemer of the enslaved, we keep this as a WATCH-NIGHT FOR ALL THE CHILDREN OF ISRAEL, dedicated to God our redeemer.

כָּל־דּוֹר וָדוֹר חַיָּב אָדָם לִרְאוֹת אֶת־עַצְמוֹ כְּאִלּוּ הוּא יָצָא מִמִּצְרָיִם. שֶׁנֶּאֱמַר וְהִגַּדְתָּ לְבִנְךָ בַּיּוֹם הַהוּא לֵאמֹר בַּעֲבוּר זֶה עָשָׂה יְיָ לִי בְּצֵאתִי מִמִּצְרָיִם: לֹא אֶת־אֲבוֹתֵינוּ בִּלְבָד גָּאַל הַקָּדוֹשׁ בָּרוּךְ הוּא. אֶלָּא אַף אוֹתָנוּ גָּאַל עִמָּהֶם. שֶׁנֶּאֱמַר וְאוֹתָנוּ הוֹצִיא מִשָּׁם לְמַעַן הָבִיא אוֹתָנוּ לָתֶת לָנוּ אֶת־הָאָרֶץ אֲשֶׁר נִשְׁבַּע לַאֲבוֹתֵינוּ:

All read in unison:

לְפִיכָךְ אֲנַחְנוּ חַיָּבִים לְהוֹדוֹת לְהַלֵּל לְשַׁבֵּחַ לְפָאֵר וּלְרוֹמֵם לְמִי שֶׁהוֹצִיא אֶת־אֲבֹתֵינוּ וְאוֹתָנוּ מֵעַבְדוּת לְחֵרוּת. מִיָּגוֹן לְשִׂמְחָה. וּמֵאֵבֶל לְיוֹם טוֹב. וּמֵאֲפֵלָה לְאוֹר גָּדוֹל. וּמִשִּׁעְבּוּד לִגְאֻלָּה. וְנֹאמַר לְפָנָיו הַלְלוּיָהּ:

While enjoying the liberty of this land, let us strive to make secure also our spiritual freedom, that, as the delivered, we may become the deliverer, carrying out Israel's historic task of being the messenger of religion unto all mankind.

All read in unison:

So it is our duty to thank, praise and glorify God, who brought us and our forefathers from slavery unto freedom, from sorrow unto joy, from mourning unto festive gladness, from darkness unto light. Let us therefore proclaim His praise.

THE EXODUS

Hallel

PSALM CXIII

Leader:

ALLELUJAH.
Praise, O ye servants of the Lord,
Praise the name of the Lord.
Company:
Blessed be the name of the Lord
From this time forth and for ever.
Leader:
From the rising of the sun unto the going down thereof
The Lord's name is to be praised.
Company:
The Lord is high above all nations,
His glory is above the heavens.
Leader:
Who is like unto the Lord our God,
That is enthroned on high,
Company:
That looketh down low
Upon heaven and upon earth?
Leader:
Who raiseth up the poor out of the dust,
And lifteth up the needy out of the dunghill;
Company:
That He may set him with princes,
Even with the princes of His people.
Leader:
Who maketh the barren woman to dwell in her house
As a joyful mother of children.
Company:
Hallelujah.

PSALM CXIII

לְלוּיָהּ:
הַלְלוּ עַבְדֵי יְיָ הַלְלוּ אֶת־שֵׁם יְיָ:
יְהִי שֵׁם יְיָ מְבֹרָךְ מֵעַתָּה וְעַד־עוֹלָם:
מִמִּזְרַח־שֶׁמֶשׁ עַד־מְבוֹאוֹ מְהֻלָּל
שֵׁם יְיָ:
רָם עַל־כָּל־גּוֹיִם יְיָ עַל הַשָּׁמַיִם כְּבוֹדוֹ:
מִי כַּיְיָ אֱלֹהֵינוּ הַמַּגְבִּיהִי לָשָׁבֶת:
הַמַּשְׁפִּילִי לִרְאוֹת בַּשָּׁמַיִם וּבָאָרֶץ:
מְקִימִי מֵעָפָר דָּל מֵאַשְׁפֹּת יָרִים אֶבְיוֹן:
לְהוֹשִׁיבִי עִם־נְדִיבִים עִם נְדִיבֵי עַמּוֹ:
מוֹשִׁיבִי עֲקֶרֶת הַבַּיִת אֵם־הַבָּנִים שְׂמֵחָה
הַלְלוּיָהּ:

*) Psalms CXIII and CXIV may be sung to the music on the following pages.

PSALM CXIV

Leader:

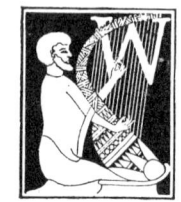

WHEN Israel came forth out of Egypt,
The house of Jacob from a people of strange language;

Company:
Judah became His sanctuary,
Israel His dominion.

Leader:
The sea saw it, and fled;
The Jordan turned backward.

Company:
The mountains skipped like rams,
The hills like young sheep.

Leader:
What aileth thee, O thou sea, that thou fleest?
Thou Jordan, that thou turnest backward?

Company:
Ye mountains that ye skip like rams;
Ye hills, like young sheep?

Leader:
Tremble, thou earth, at the presence of the Lord,
At the presence of the God of Jacob;

Company:
Who turned the rock into a pool of water,
The flint into a fountain of waters.

PSALM CXIV

צֵאת יִשְׂרָאֵל מִמִּצְרָיִם בֵּית יַעֲקֹב
מֵעַם לֹעֵז:
הָיְתָה יְהוּדָה לְקָדְשׁוֹ יִשְׂרָאֵל
מַמְשְׁלוֹתָיו:
הַיָּם רָאָה וַיָּנֹס הַיַּרְדֵּן יִסֹּב לְאָחוֹר:
הֶהָרִים רָקְדוּ כְאֵילִים גְּבָעוֹת כִּבְנֵי־צֹאן:
מַה־לְּךָ הַיָּם כִּי תָנוּס הַיַּרְדֵּן תִּסֹּב לְאָחוֹר:
הֶהָרִים תִּרְקְדוּ כְאֵילִים גְּבָעוֹת כִּבְנֵי־צֹאן:
מִלִּפְנֵי אָדוֹן חוּלִי אָרֶץ מִלִּפְנֵי אֱלוֹהַּ יַעֲקֹב:
הַהֹפְכִי הַצּוּר אֲגַם־מָיִם חַלָּמִישׁ לְמַעְיְנוֹ־מָיִם:

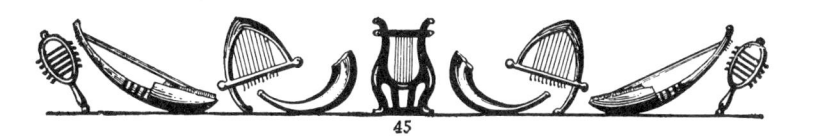

Psalm CXIII

Traditional Chant

1. Ha-la-lu av-de a-do-noi...... ha-la-lu es shem ado-noi 2. Y'hi shem a-do-noi m'vo-roch me-at-to v'ad o-lom.
3. Mimmiz-rah she-mesh ad m'vo-o.......... m'hul-lol shem ado-noi 4. Rom al kol go-yim ado-noi al hashsho-mayim k'vo-do.
5. Mi ka-do-noi e-lo-he-nu ham-mag-bi hi lo-sho-ves 6. Hammash-pi-li lir-os bashsho-mayim u-vo-o-retz.
7. M'-ki-mi me-o-for........... dol....... me-ash-pos yo-rim ev-yon 8. L'ho-shi-vi im n'di-vim im............ n'di-ve am-mo.
9. Mo-shi-vi a-ke-res hab-ba-yis em hab-bo-nim s'me-hoh 10. Ha-la-lu-yoh Ha-la-lu-yoh.

46

Psalm CXIV

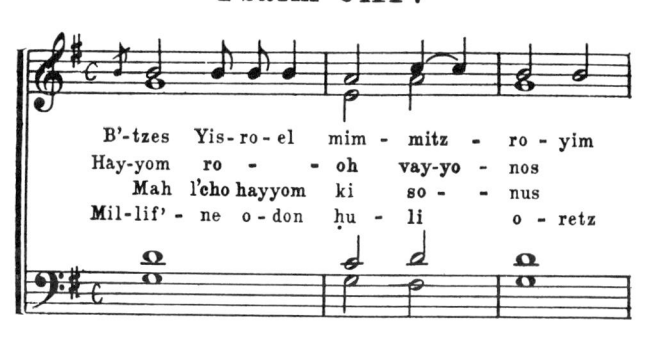

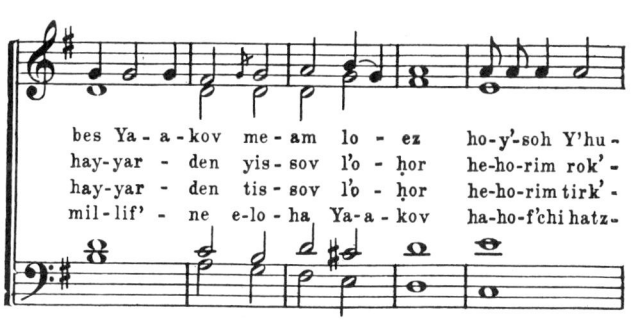

B'-tzes Yis-ro-el mim- mitz - ro-yim bes Ya-a-kov me-am lo - ez ho-y'-soh Y'hu-doh l'-kod-sho Yis-ro-el mamsh'lo-sov.

Hay-yom ro - - oh vay-yo - nos hay-yar - den yis-sov l'o - ḥor he-ho-rim rok'- du ch'-e - lim g'vo - os kiv-ne tzon.

Mah l'cho hayyom ki so - - nus hay-yar - den tis-sov l'o - ḥor he-ho-rim tirk'- du ch'-e - lim g'vo - os kiv-ne tzon.

Mil-lif' - ne o-don ḥu - li o - retz mil-lif' - ne e-lo-ha Ya-a-kov ha-ho-f'chi hatz- tzur a-gam mo-yim ḥal-lo - mish l'-ma-y'no mo-yim.

Blessings

PRAISED art Thou, O Lord our God, King of the universe, who hast redeemed us and our ancestors from Egypt, and hast enabled us to observe this night of the Passover, the Feast of Unleavened Bread. O Lord our God and God of our fathers, may we, with Thy help, live to celebrate other feasts and holy seasons. May we rejoice in Thy salvation and be gladdened by Thy righteousness. Grant deliverance to mankind through Israel, Thy people. May Thy will be done through Jacob, Thy chosen servant, so that Thy name shall be sanctified in the midst of all the earth, and that all peoples be moved to worship Thee with one accord. And we shall sing new songs of praise unto Thee, for our redemption and for the deliverance of our souls. Praised art Thou, O God, Redeemer of Israel.

The cups are filled for the second time.

All read in unison:

BORUCH ATTO ADONOI ELOHENU MELECH HO'OLOM BORE P'RI HAGGOFEN.

Praised art Thou, O Lord our God, King of the universe, who hast created the fruit of the vine.

Drink the second cup of wine.

בָּרוּךְ אַתָּה יְיָ אֱלֹהֵינוּ מֶלֶךְ הָעוֹלָם. אֲשֶׁר גְּאָלָנוּ וְגָאַל אֶת־אֲבוֹתֵינוּ מִמִּצְרָיִם. וְהִגִּיעָנוּ הַלַּיְלָה הַזֶּה לֶאֱכָל־בּוֹ מַצָּה וּמָרוֹר. כֵּן יְיָ אֱלֹהֵינוּ וֵאלֹהֵי אֲבוֹתֵינוּ יַגִּיעֵנוּ לְמוֹעֲדִים וְלִרְגָלִים אֲחֵרִים הַבָּאִים לִקְרָאתֵנוּ לְשָׁלוֹם. שְׂמֵחִים בְּיִשׁוּעָתֶךָ. וְשָׂשִׂים בְּצִדְקָתֶךָ. וְנִזְכֶּה לִרְאוֹת בְּהִגָּלוֹת זְרָעֶךָ עַל יִשְׂרָאֵל עַמֶּךָ. וְחֶפְצְךָ יִצְלַח בְּיַד יַעֲקֹב עַבְדְּךָ בְחִירֶךָ. יִתְקַדַּשׁ שִׁמְךָ בְּתוֹךְ כָּל הָאָרֶץ. וְיַעַבְדוּךָ עַמִּים שְׁכֶם אֶחָד. וְנוֹדֶה־לְךָ שִׁיר חָדָשׁ עַל־גְּאֻלָּתֵנוּ וְעַל פְּדוּת נַפְשֵׁנוּ: בָּרוּךְ אַתָּה יְיָ. גָּאַל יִשְׂרָאֵל:

The cups are filled for the second time.

All read in unison:

בָּרוּךְ אַתָּה יְיָ אֱלֹהֵינוּ מֶלֶךְ הָעוֹלָם בּוֹרֵא פְּרִי הַגָּפֶן:

Drink the second cup of wine.

5. מוֹצִיא, מַצָּה

The upper Matzo is broken and distributed. All then read in unison:

BORUCH ATTO ADONOI ELOHENU MELECH HO'OLOM HAMOTZI LEHEM MIN HO'ORETZ.

Praised art Thou, O Lord our God, King of the universe, who bringest forth bread from the earth.

BORUCH ATTO ADONOI ELOHENU MELECH HO'OLOM ASHER KIDD'SHONU B'MITZVOSOV V'TZIVONU AL ACHILAS MATZO.

Praised art Thou, O Lord our God, King of the universe, who hast sanctified us through Thy commandments, and ordained that we should eat unleavened bread.

Eat the Matzo.

6. כּוֹרֵךְ, מָרוֹר

Each person receives some bitter herbs and haroses, which he places between two pieces of matzo. The leader then reads:

This was the practice of Hillel, at the time the Temple was still in existence. He combined the unleavened bread and the bitter herbs and ate them together, to carry out the injunction concerning the Passover sacrifice: "With unleavened bread and with bitter herbs, they shall eat it."

All read in unison:

BORUCH ATTO ADONOI ELOHENU MELECH HO'OLOM ASHER KIDD'SHONU B'MITZVOSOV V'TZIVONU AL ACHILAS MOROR.

Praised art Thou, O Lord our God, King of the universe, who hast sanctified us by Thy commandments, and ordained that we should eat bitter herbs.

Eat the Moror.

5. מוֹצִיא, מַצָּה

The upper Matzo is broken and distributed. All then read in unison:

בָּרוּךְ אַתָּה יְיָ אֱלֹהֵינוּ מֶלֶךְ הָעוֹלָם. הַמּוֹצִיא לֶחֶם מִן־הָאָרֶץ:

בָּרוּךְ אַתָּה יְיָ. אֱלֹהֵינוּ מֶלֶךְ הָעוֹלָם. אֲשֶׁר קִדְּשָׁנוּ בְּמִצְוֹתָיו וְצִוָּנוּ עַל־אֲכִילַת מַצָּה:

Eat the Matzo.

6. כּוֹרֵךְ, מָרוֹר

Each person receives some bitter herbs and haroses which he places between two pieces of matzo. The leader then reads:

כֵּן עָשָׂה הִלֵּל בִּזְמַן שֶׁבֵּית הַמִּקְדָּשׁ הָיָה קַיָּם. הָיָה כּוֹרֵךְ מַצָּה וּמָרוֹר וְאוֹכֵל בְּיַחַד. לְקַיֵּם מַה שֶׁנֶּאֱמַר עַל־מַצּוֹת וּמְרוֹרִים יֹאכְלֻהוּ:

All read in unison:

בָּרוּךְ אַתָּה יְיָ אֱלֹהֵינוּ מֶלֶךְ הָעוֹלָם. אֲשֶׁר קִדְּשָׁנוּ בְּמִצְוֹתָיו וְצִוָּנוּ עַל־אֲכִילַת מָרוֹר:

Eat the Moror.

7. שֻׁלְחָן עוֹרֵךְ

SUPPER IS SERVED.

8. צָפוּן

Partake of the Aphikomon.

At the conclusion of the meal, the children are given an opportunity to find the Aphikomon. The reader redeems it and distributes pieces of it to all present.

After partaking of the Aphikomon, it is customary to eat nothing else.

B. After the Meal

To Thee Above

Thee a - bove all crea - tures' gaze, To Thee whom earth and heav'n do praise, Whose
didst re - deem the cap - tive band Who were en - slaved by ty - rant's hand. Their
God, Thy chil - dren rec - og - nize With grate - ful hearts this pre - cious prize. Thy

ev - er watch-ful prov - i - dence Proves dai-ly Thine om-
cries were heard, their groans were still'd, Their yearning hopes at
peo-ple at this fes - tive time Pro-claim a-loud Thy

ni - po-tence, To Thee our thanks in
last ful-filled, And Free_ dom dawned on
grace sub-lime. The Lord will reign for

|1 & 2| |3|

cho - rus rise. 2. Thou
Is - ra - el. 3. O
ev - er - more

Grace after the Meal

9. בָּרֵךְ

Leader:

LET US say grace.

Company:

Let us bless Him of whose bounty we have partaken and through whose goodness we live.

Leader:

Praised art Thou, O Lord our God, King of the universe, who sustainest the world with goodness, with grace, and with infinite mercy. Thou givest food unto every creature, for Thy mercy endureth for ever.

Company:

Through Thy great goodness, food has not failed us. May it never fail us at any time, for the sake of Thy great name.

Leader:

Thou sustainest and dealest graciously with all Thy creatures.

Company:

Praised art Thou, O Lord, who givest food unto all.

All read in unison:

O God, our Father, sustain and protect us and grant us strength to bear our burdens. Let us not, O God, become dependent upon men, but let us rather depend

9. בָּרֵךְ

Leader:

בּוֹתַי נְבָרֵךְ לֵאלֹהֵינוּ שֶׁאָכַלְנוּ מִשֶּׁלוֹ:

Company:

בָּרוּךְ אֱלֹהֵינוּ שֶׁאָכַלְנוּ מִשֶּׁלוֹ וּבְטוּבוֹ חָיִינוּ:

Leader:

בָּרוּךְ אֱלֹהֵינוּ שֶׁאָכַלְנוּ מִשֶּׁלוֹ וּבְטוּבוֹ חָיִינוּ:

בָּרוּךְ אַתָּה יְיָ אֱלֹהֵינוּ מֶלֶךְ הָעוֹלָם. הַזָּן אֶת־הָעוֹלָם כֻּלּוֹ בְּטוּבוֹ בְּחֵן בְּחֶסֶד וּבְרַחֲמִים. הוּא נוֹתֵן לֶחֶם לְכָל־בָּשָׂר. כִּי לְעוֹלָם חַסְדּוֹ. וּבְטוּבוֹ הַגָּדוֹל תָּמִיד לֹא־חָסַר לָנוּ וְאַל יֶחְסַר־לָנוּ מָזוֹן לְעוֹלָם וָעֶד. בַּעֲבוּר שְׁמוֹ הַגָּדוֹל. כִּי הוּא זָן וּמְפַרְנֵס לַכֹּל. וּמֵטִיב לַכֹּל. וּמֵכִין מָזוֹן לְכָל בְּרִיּוֹתָיו אֲשֶׁר בָּרָא: בָּרוּךְ אַתָּה יְיָ הַזָּן אֶת־הַכֹּל:

All read in unison:

אֱלֹהֵינוּ אָבִינוּ. רְעֵנוּ זוּנֵנוּ. פַּרְנְסֵנוּ וְכַלְכְּלֵנוּ. וְהַרְוִיחֵנוּ. וְהַרְוַח־לָנוּ יְיָ אֱלֹהֵינוּ מְהֵרָה מִכָּל־צָרוֹתֵינוּ. וְנָא אַל־תַּצְרִיכֵנוּ יְיָ אֱלֹהֵינוּ לֹא לִידֵי

upon Thy hand, which is ever open and gracious, so that we may never be put to shame.

Leader:

Our God and God of our fathers, be Thou ever mindful of us, as Thou hast been of our fathers, so that we may find enlargement, grace, mercy, life and peace on this Feast of Unleavened Bread.

Company: AMEN

Remember us this day in kindness.

Company: AMEN

Visit us this day with blessing.

Company: AMEN

Preserve us this day for life.

Company: AMEN

With Thy saving and gracious word have mercy upon us and save us, for unto Thee, the compassionate and merciful One, our eyes are ever turned, for Thou art a gracious and merciful King.

The All-merciful! May He reign over us for ever!

Company: AMEN

The All-merciful! May He sustain us in honor!

Company: AMEN

The All-merciful! May He bless this household and all assembled here. May we all find favor in the eyes of God and men!

Company: AMEN

מַתְּנַת בָּשָׂר וָדָם וְלֹא לִידֵי הַלְוָאָתָם. כִּי אִם לְיָדְךָ הַמְּלֵאָה הַפְּתוּחָה הַקְּדוּשָׁה וְהָרְחָבָה. שֶׁלֹּא-נֵבוֹשׁ וְלֹא-נִכָּלֵם לְעוֹלָם וָעֶד:

Leader:

אֱלֹהֵינוּ וֵאלֹהֵי אֲבוֹתֵינוּ. יַעֲלֶה וְיָבֹא וְיַפְקֵד וְיִזָּכֵר זִכְרוֹנֵנוּ וְזִכְרוֹן אֲבוֹתֵינוּ. וְזִכְרוֹן עַמְּךָ יִשְׂרָאֵל מְשִׁיחַךְ לְפָנֶיךָ. לִפְלֵטָה וּלְטוֹבָה וּלְחֵן וּלְחֶסֶד וּלְרַחֲמִים וּלְחַיִּים וּלְשָׁלוֹם בְּיוֹם חַג הַמַּצּוֹת הַזֶּה.

זָכְרֵנוּ יְיָ אֱלֹהֵינוּ בּוֹ לְטוֹבָה. אָמֵן.
וּפָקְדֵנוּ בוֹ לִבְרָכָה. אָמֵן.
וְהוֹשִׁיעֵנוּ בוֹ לְחַיִּים. אָמֵן.

וּבִדְבַר יְשׁוּעָה וְרַחֲמִים חוּס וְחָנֵּנוּ וְרַחֵם עָלֵינוּ וְהוֹשִׁיעֵנוּ כִּי אֵלֶיךָ עֵינֵינוּ. כִּי אֵל מֶלֶךְ חַנּוּן וְרַחוּם אָתָּה:

הָרַחֲמָן. הוּא יִמְלוֹךְ עָלֵינוּ לְעוֹלָם וָעֶד: הָרַחֲמָן הוּא יְפַרְנְסֵנוּ בְּכָבוֹד: הָרַחֲמָן הוּא יִשְׁלַח בְּרָכָה מְרֻבָּה בַּבַּיִת הַזֶּה וְעַל-שֻׁלְחָן זֶה שֶׁאָכַלְנוּ עָלָיו: הָרַחֲמָן הוּא יְבָרֵךְ [אֶת-אָבִי מוֹרִי בַּעַל הַבַּיִת הַזֶּה וְאֶת-אִמִּי מוֹרָתִי בַּעֲלַת הַבַּיִת הַזֶּה וְאֶת אוֹתָם וְאֶת בֵּיתָם וְאֶת-זַרְעָם וְאֶת-כָּל אֲשֶׁר לָהֶם] אוֹתָנוּ וְאֶת-כָּל-אֲשֶׁר

Leader:

Fear ye the Lord, ye His holy ones, for there is no want to them that fear Him.

Company:

The young lions do lack and suffer hunger, but they that seek the Lord shall not lack any good thing.

Leader:

O give thanks unto the Lord, for He is good, for His mercy endureth for ever.

Company:

Thou openest Thy hand and satisfiest every living thing with favor.

Leader:

Blessed is the man that trusteth in the Lord; the Lord shall be unto him for a help.

Company:

The Lord will give strength unto His people;
The Lord will bless His people with peace.

The cups are filled for the third time.

All read in unison:

BORUCH ATTO ADONOI ELOHENU MELECH HO'OLOM BORE P'RI HAGGOFEN.

Blessed art Thou, O Lord our God, King of the universe, who createst the fruit of the vine.

Drink the third cup of wine.

לָנוּ. וְנִשָּׂא בְרָכָה מֵאֵת יְיָ וּצְדָקָה מֵאֱלֹהֵי יִשְׁעֵנוּ:
וְנִמְצָא־חֵן וְשֵׂכֶל טוֹב בְּעֵינֵי אֱלֹהִים וְאָדָם:

Leader:
יְראוּ אֶת יְיָ קְדֹשָׁיו כִּי אֵין מַחְסוֹר לִירֵאָיו:

Company:
כְּפִירִים רָשׁוּ וְרָעֵבוּ וְדֹרְשֵׁי יְיָ לֹא־יַחְסְרוּ כָל־טוֹב:

Leader:
הוֹדוּ לַיְיָ כִּי־טוֹב כִּי לְעוֹלָם חַסְדּוֹ:

Company:
פּוֹתֵחַ אֶת יָדֶךָ וּמַשְׂבִּיעַ לְכָל־חַי רָצוֹן:

Leader:
בָּרוּךְ הַגֶּבֶר אֲשֶׁר יִבְטַח בַּיְיָ וְהָיָה יְיָ מִבְטַחוֹ:

Company:
יְיָ עֹז לְעַמּוֹ יִתֵּן יְיָ יְבָרֵךְ אֶת־עַמּוֹ בַשָּׁלוֹם:

The cups are filled for the third time.

All read in unison:
בָּרוּךְ אַתָּה יְיָ אֱלֹהֵינוּ מֶלֶךְ הָעוֹלָם בּוֹרֵא פְּרִי הַגָּפֶן:

Drink the third cup of wine.

10. הַלֵּל

THE DOOR IS OPENED FOR ELIJAH

PSALM CXVII

Leader:
PRAISE the Lord, all ye nations;
Company:
Laud Him, all ye peoples.
Leader:
For His mercy is great toward us;
Company:
And the truth of the Lord endureth for ever. Hallelujah!

THE DOOR IS CLOSED.

PSALM CXVIII: 1-4

Leader:
O give thanks unto the Lord, for He is good,
Company:
For His mercy endureth for ever.
Leader:
So let Israel now say,
Company:
For His mercy endureth for ever.
Leader:
So let the house of Aaron now say,
Company:
For His mercy endureth for ever.
Leader:
So let them now that fear the Lord say,
Company:
For His mercy endureth for ever.

10. הַלֵּל

THE DOOR IS OPENED FOR ELIJAH.

PSALM CXVII*

לְלוּ אֶת־יְיָ כָּל־גּוֹיִם שַׁבְּחוּהוּ כָּל־הָאֻמִּים: כִּי גָבַר עָלֵינוּ חַסְדּוֹ וֶאֱמֶת יְיָ לְעוֹלָם. הַלְלוּיָהּ:

THE DOOR IS CLOSED.

PSALM CXVIII: 1-4

הוֹדוּ לַיְיָ כִּי־טוֹב   כִּי לְעוֹלָם חַסְדּוֹ:

יֹאמַר־נָא יִשְׂרָאֵל   כִּי לְעוֹלָם חַסְדּוֹ:

יֹאמְרוּ־נָא בֵית־אַהֲרֹן   כִּי לְעוֹלָם חַסְדּוֹ:

יֹאמְרוּ־נָא יִרְאֵי יְיָ   כִּי לְעוֹלָם חַסְדּוֹ:

Psalm CXVII and CXVIII may be sung to the music on the following pages.

Psalm CXVII

First Tune

SOLO

Ha - la - lu es a - do - noi kol go - yim

Shab - b' - hu - hu kol ho - um - mim.

CHORUS

Ki go - var o - le - nu has - do

ve - e - mes a - do - noi l' - o - lom, ha - l' - lu - yoh.

Psalm CXVII

Second Tune — Traditional

Ha-la-lu es ado-noi kol go-yim
shab-b'-hu-hu kol ho-um-mim
Ki go-var o-le-nu has-do ve-e-mes ado-noi l'-o-lom Ha-l'lu-yoh.

Hodu Ladonoi

CHOR.

Ho - du la-do - noi ki - - tov ki l'o - lom..... has - - do

SOLO

Yo - mar no......... yis - - ro - el

ki - l' - o - lom has - - do

CHOR.
Ho - du la-do - noi.... ki - - tov....

ki - l'o - lom.... has - - do.

SOLO
Yom'- ru - no — bes — a - ha-ron ki - l'-
CHOR.
o - lom ḥas - - do — Ho - du la-do - noi...
ki - - tov ki l'o- lom ḥas - do

SOLO
Yom-ru no........ yir'-e ado-noi ki l'-
o-lom has - - do....
CHOR.
Ho-du la-do-noi
ki....... tov ki l'-o-lom has - do.

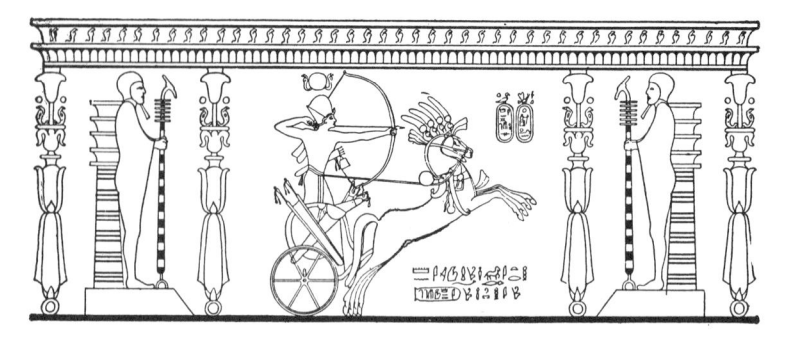

PSALM CXVIII: 5-29

Leader:

OUT OF distress I called upon the Lord; He answered me with great enlargement.

Company:

The Lord is for me; I will not fear; what can man do unto me?

Leader:

It is better to take refuge in the Lord than to trust in man.

Company:

It is better to take refuge in the Lord than to trust in princes.

Leader:

The Lord is my strength and song; and He is become my salvation.

Company:

The voice of rejoicing and salvation is in the tents of the righteous.

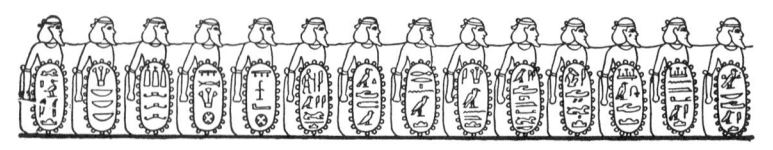

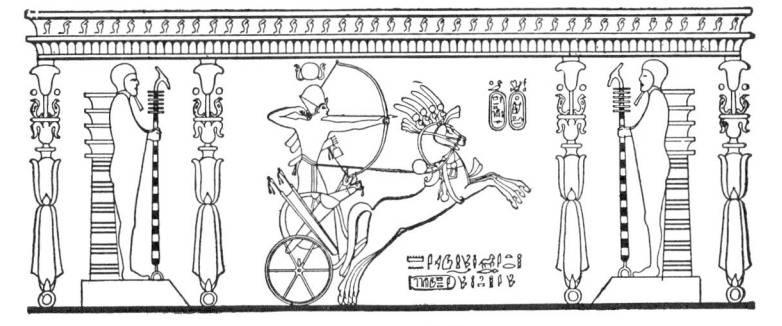

PSALM CXVIII: 5–29

וְהַמֵּצַר קָרָאתִי יָּהּ עָנָנִי
בַמֶּרְחָב יָהּ:
יְיָ לִי לֹא אִירָא מַה־יַּעֲשֶׂה לִי
אָדָם:
יְיָ לִי בְּעֹזְרָי וַאֲנִי אֶרְאֶה בְשֹׂנְאָי:
טוֹב לַחֲסוֹת בַּיְיָ מִבְּטֹחַ בָּאָדָם:
טוֹב לַחֲסוֹת בַּיְיָ מִבְּטֹחַ בִּנְדִיבִים:
כָּל־גּוֹיִם סְבָבוּנִי בְּשֵׁם יְיָ כִּי אֲמִילַם:
סַבּוּנִי גַם סְבָבוּנִי בְּשֵׁם יְיָ כִּי אֲמִילַם:
סַבּוּנִי כִדְבֹרִים דֹּעֲכוּ כְּאֵשׁ קוֹצִים בְּשֵׁם יְיָ כִּי
אֲמִילַם:
דָּחֹה דְחִיתַנִי לִנְפֹּל וַיְיָ עֲזָרָנִי:

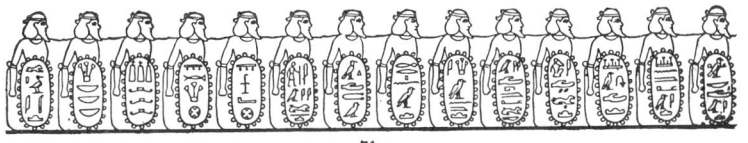

Leader:

The right hand of the Lord doeth valiantly; the right hand of the Lord is exalted.

Company:

I shall not die but live, and declare the works of the Lord.

Leader:

The Lord hath chastened me sore; but He hath not given me over unto death.

Company:

Open to me the gates of righteousness; I will enter into them; I will give thanks unto the Lord.

Leader:

This is the gate of the Lord; the righteous shall enter into it.

Company:

I will give thanks unto Thee, for Thou hast answered me, and art become my salvation.

Leader:

The stone which the builders rejected is become the chief corner-stone.

Company:

This is the Lord's doing; it is marvelous in our eyes.

Leader:

This is the day which the Lord hath made; we will rejoice and be glad in it.

Company:

We beseech Thee, O Lord, save now! We beseech Thee, O Lord, make us now to prosper!

Leader:

Blessed be he that cometh in the name of the Lord;

עָזִּי וְזִמְרָת יָהּ וַיְהִי־לִי לִישׁוּעָה:

קוֹל רִנָּה וִישׁוּעָה בְּאָהֳלֵי צַדִּיקִים יְמִין יְיָ עֹשָׂה חָיִל:

יְמִין יְיָ רוֹמֵמָה יְמִין יְיָ עֹשָׂה חָיִל:

לֹא־אָמוּת כִּי־אֶחְיֶה וַאֲסַפֵּר מַעֲשֵׂי יָהּ:

יַסֹּר יִסְּרַנִּי יָּהּ וְלַמָּוֶת לֹא נְתָנָנִי:

פִּתְחוּ־לִי שַׁעֲרֵי־צֶדֶק אָבֹא־בָם אוֹדֶה יָהּ:

זֶה־הַשַּׁעַר לַיְיָ צַדִּיקִים יָבֹאוּ בוֹ:

אוֹדְךָ כִּי עֲנִיתָנִי וַתְּהִי־לִי לִישׁוּעָה:

אֶבֶן מָאֲסוּ הַבּוֹנִים הָיְתָה לְרֹאשׁ פִּנָּה:

מֵאֵת יְיָ הָיְתָה זֹּאת הִיא נִפְלָאת בְּעֵינֵינוּ:

*זֶה־הַיּוֹם עָשָׂה יְיָ נָגִילָה וְנִשְׂמְחָה בוֹ:

אָנָּא יְיָ הוֹשִׁיעָה נָּא:

אָנָּא יְיָ הוֹשִׁיעָה נָּא:

אָנָּא יְיָ הַצְלִיחָה נָא:

אָנָּא יְיָ הַצְלִיחָה נָּא:

בָּרוּךְ הַבָּא בְּשֵׁם יְיָ בֵּרַכְנוּכֶם מִבֵּית יְיָ:

*) These verses may be sung to the music on the following pages.

Company:
We bless you out of the house of the Lord.
Leader:
Thou art my God, and I will give thanks unto Thee;
Company:
Thou art my God, I will exalt Thee.
Leader:
O give thanks unto the Lord, for He is good,
Company:
For His mercy endureth for ever.

אֵל יְיָ וַיָּאֶר לָנוּ אִסְרוּ־חַג בַּעֲבֹתִים עַד־קַרְנוֹת הַמִּזְבֵּחַ:
אֵלִי אַתָּה וְאוֹדֶךָּ אֱלֹהַי אֲרוֹמְמֶךָּ:
הוֹדוּ לַיְיָ כִּי־טוֹב כִּי לְעוֹלָם חַסְדּוֹ:

Zeh Hayom

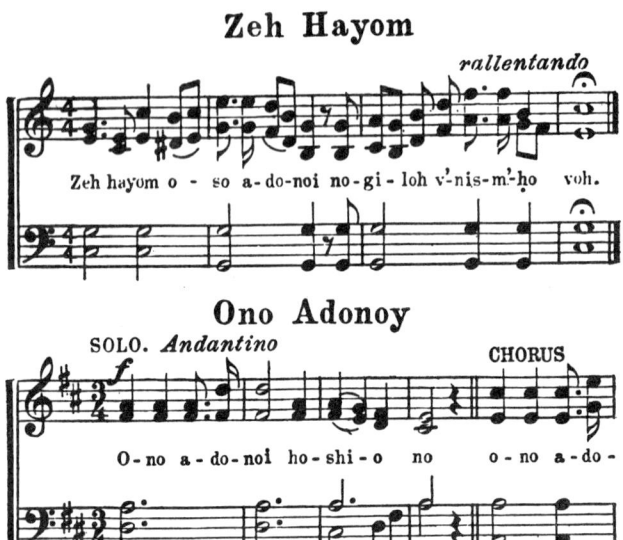

Zeh hayom o - so a-do-noi no-gi-loh v'-nis-m'-ho voh.

Ono Adonoy

SOLO. Andantino

O-no a-do-noi ho-shi-o no o-no a-do-noi ho-shi-o no o-no a-do-noi hatz-li-ho no o-no a-do-noi hatz-li-ho no.

Hodu Ladonoi

Ho - du la-do - noi ki tov ki........ l'-o-lom has-do ki l'-o-lom has - do.

11. נִרְצָה
The Final Benediction

The cups are filled for the fourth time.
The leader lifts the cup of wine and reads:

THE FESTIVE service is completed. With songs of praise, we have lifted up the cups symbolizing the divine promises of salvation, and have called upon the name of God. As we offer the benediction over the fourth cup, let us again lift our souls to God in faith and in hope. May He who broke Pharaoh's yoke for ever shatter all fetters of oppression, and hasten the day when swords shall, at last, be broken and wars ended. Soon may He cause the glad tidings of redemption to be heard in all lands, so that mankind — freed from violence and from wrong, and united in an eternal covenant of brotherhood — may celebrate the universal Passover in the name of our God of freedom.

All read in unison:

May God bless the whole house of Israel with freedom, and keep us safe from danger everywhere. Amen.

May God cause the light of His countenance to shine upon all men, and dispel the darkness of ignorance and of prejudice. May He be gracious unto us.
Amen.

May God lift up His countenance upon our country and render it a true home of liberty and a bulwark of justice. And may He grant peace unto us and unto all mankind. Amen.

בָּרוּךְ אַתָּה יְיָ אֱלֹהֵינוּ מֶלֶךְ הָעוֹלָם בּוֹרֵא פְּרִי הַגֶּפֶן:

BORUCH ATTO ADONOI ELOHENU MELECH HO'OLOM BORE P'RI HAGGOFEN.

Praised art Thou, O Lord our God, King of the universe, who createst the fruit of the vine.

Drink the fourth cup of wine.

God of Might

Traditional "Addir Hu"

CHORUS. *Maestoso*

1. God of might, God of right, Thee we give all glo - ry;
   Thine all praise in these days As in a - ges hoar - y,
   When we hear, year by year, Free-dom's wondrous sto - ry.
2. Now as erst, when Thou first Mad'st the proc-la - ma - tion,
   Warning loud ev-'ry proud, Ev-'ry ty - rant na - tion,
   We Thy fame still proclaim, Bow'd in a - do - ra - tion.
3. Be with all who in thrall To their tasks are driv - en;
   By Thy power speed the hour When their chains are riv - en;
   Earth a-round will resound Joy-ful hymns to heav - en.

80

Addir Hu

Traditional

CHORUS. *Maestoso*

1. Addir hu, addir hu, yivneh ve-so b'- ko-rov,
2. Boḥur hu, godol hu, yoḥid hu, *(Refrain)*
3. Tzaddik hu, kodosh hu, raḥum hu, *(Refrain)*

bim'-he-roh,— bim'-he-roh b'-yo-me-nu b'-ko-rov,

el b'-ne, el b'-ne, b'ne ves'-cho b'-ko-rov.

Our Souls We Raise In Fervent Praise

CHORUS. *Andante con moto* Traditional Ki Lo Noeh

Our souls we raise in fer-vent praise.

SOLO

1. Lo! glo-rious is the reign, Thy law and love sus-tain, Earth ech-oes Heaven's re-frain:
2. Es-tab-lished is Thy throne, Thou rul-est, one, a-lone, The na-tions all in-tone:
3. Lo! boundless is Thy power, Our Rock and shelt'ring tow'r! Thy grace on Is-rael shower,

CHORUS

To Thee, O to Thee, To

Thee, yea to Thee, To Thee, might - y Lord, Be -
long the vic - to - ry and ma - jes - ty. Our
souls we raise in fer - vent praise.
f

Ki Lo Noeh

Traditional

CHORUS. *Andante con moto*

Ki lo no - eh Ki lo yo - eh.

SOLO

1. Ad - dir bim'-lu - cho, bo - hur ka-ha-lo - cho, g'-
2. Ko - dosh bim'-lu - cho, ra - hum ka-ha-lo - cho, shin-
3. Tak - kif bim'-lu - cho, to - mech ka-ha-lo - cho, t'-

CHORUS

du - dov yom'- ru lo,
a - nov yom'- ru lo, l' - cho u - l'- cho, l' -
mi - mov yom'- ru lo,

cho ki l'-cho l' - cho af l'-cho l' -
cho a - do - noi ham - mam - lo - cho, Ki
lo no - eh, ki lo yo - eh.
f

A Madrigal of Numbers

The leader asks the questions. The whole company responds, each reading as fast as possible, in the effort to finish the answer first.

Who knows One?

I know One: One is the God of the World.

Who knows Two?

I know Two: Two Tables of the Covenant. One God of the World.

Who knows Three?

I know Three: Three Patriarchs; Two Tables of the Covenant; One God of the World.

Who knows Four?

I know Four: Four Mothers of Israel; Three Patriarchs; Two Tables of the Covenant; One God of the World.

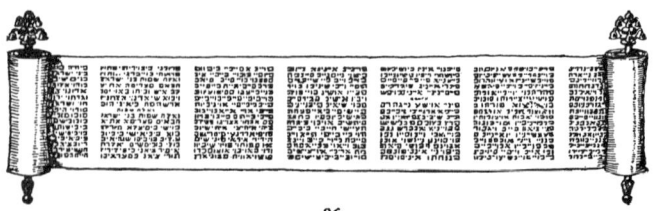

אֶחָד מִי יוֹדֵעַ?

אֶחָד אֲנִי יוֹדֵעַ. אֶחָד אֱלֹהֵינוּ שֶׁבַּשָּׁמַיִם וּבָאָרֶץ:

שְׁנַיִם מִי יוֹדֵעַ?

שְׁנַיִם אֲנִי יוֹדֵעַ. שְׁנֵי לֻחוֹת הַבְּרִית. אֶחָד אֱלֹהֵינוּ שֶׁבַּשָּׁמַיִם וּבָאָרֶץ:

שְׁלֹשָׁה מִי יוֹדֵעַ?

שְׁלֹשָׁה אֲנִי יוֹדֵעַ: שְׁלֹשָׁה אָבוֹת. שְׁנֵי לֻחוֹת הַבְּרִית. אֶחָד אֱלֹהֵינוּ שֶׁבַּשָּׁמַיִם וּבָאָרֶץ:

אַרְבַּע מִי יוֹדֵעַ?

אַרְבַּע אֲנִי יוֹדֵעַ. אַרְבַּע אִמָּהוֹת. שְׁלֹשָׁה אָבוֹת. שְׁנֵי לֻחוֹת הַבְּרִית. אֶחָד אֱלֹהֵינוּ שֶׁבַּשָּׁמַיִם וּבָאָרֶץ:

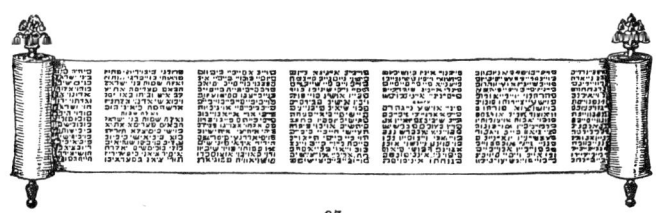

Who knows Five?

I know Five: Five Books of Moses; Four Mothers of Israel; Three Patriarchs; Two Tables of the Covenant; One God of the World.

Who knows Six?

I know Six: Six Days of Creation; Five Books of Moses; Four Mothers of Israel; Three Patriarchs; Two Tables of the Covenant; One God of the World.

Who knows Seven?

I know Seven: Seven Days of the Week; Six Days of Creation; Five Books of Moses; Four Mothers of Israel; Three Patriarchs; Two Tables of the Covenant; One God of the World.

Who knows Eight?

I know Eight: Eight Lights of Ḥanukkah; Seven Days of the Week; Six Days of Creation; Five Books of Moses; Four Mothers of Israel; Three Patriarchs; Two Tables of the Covenant; One God of the World.

Who knows Nine?

I know Nine: Nine Festivals*; Eight Lights of

* The nine Jewish festivals are: 1. Pesaḥ (Passover), 2. Shabuoth (Feast of Weeks, or Pentecost) 3. Rosh Hashanah (New Year) 4. Yom Kippur (Day of Atonement) 5. Succoth (Feast of Tabernacles) 6. Sh'mini Atzereth (Eighth Day of Solemn Assembly) 7. Simḥath Torah (Rejoicing in the Law), 8. Ḥanukkah (Feast of Dedication or Feast of Lights) 9. Purim (Feast of Lots)

חֲמִשָּׁה מִי יוֹדֵעַ?

חֲמִשָּׁה אֲנִי יוֹדֵעַ. חֲמִשָּׁה חֻמְשֵׁי תוֹרָה. אַרְבַּע אִמָּהוֹת. שְׁלֹשָׁה אָבוֹת. שְׁנֵי לֻחוֹת הַבְּרִית. אֶחָד אֱלֹהֵינוּ שֶׁבַּשָּׁמַיִם וּבָאָרֶץ:

שִׁשָּׁה מִי יוֹדֵעַ?

שִׁשָּׁה אֲנִי יוֹדֵעַ. שִׁשָּׁה סִדְרֵי מִשְׁנָה. חֲמִשָּׁה חֻמְשֵׁי תוֹרָה. אַרְבַּע אִמָּהוֹת. שְׁלֹשָׁה אָבוֹת. שְׁנֵי לֻחוֹת הַבְּרִית. אֶחָד אֱלֹהֵינוּ שֶׁבַּשָּׁמַיִם וּבָאָרֶץ:

שִׁבְעָה מִי יוֹדֵעַ?

שִׁבְעָה אֲנִי יוֹדֵעַ. שִׁבְעָה יְמֵי שַׁבַּתָּא. שִׁשָּׁה סִדְרֵי מִשְׁנָה. חֲמִשָּׁה חֻמְשֵׁי תוֹרָה. אַרְבַּע אִמָּהוֹת. שְׁלֹשָׁה אָבוֹת. שְׁנֵי לֻחוֹת הַבְּרִית. אֶחָד אֱלֹהֵינוּ שֶׁבַּשָּׁמַיִם וּבָאָרֶץ:

שְׁמוֹנָה מִי יוֹדֵעַ?

שְׁמוֹנָה אֲנִי יוֹדֵעַ. שְׁמוֹנָה יְמֵי חֲנֻכָּה. שִׁבְעָה יְמֵי שַׁבַּתָּא. שִׁשָּׁה סִדְרֵי מִשְׁנָה. חֲמִשָּׁה חֻמְשֵׁי תוֹרָה. אַרְבַּע אִמָּהוֹת. שְׁלֹשָׁה אָבוֹת. שְׁנֵי לֻחוֹת הַבְּרִית. אֶחָד אֱלֹהֵיוּ שֶׁבַּשָּׁמַיִם וּבָאָרֶץ:

תִּשְׁעָה מִי יוֹדֵעַ?

תִּשְׁעָה אֲנִי יוֹדֵעַ. תִּשְׁעָה זְמַנֵּי שִׂמְחָה. שְׁמוֹנָה

Hanukkah; Seven Days of the Week; Six Days of Creation; Five Books of Moses; Four Mothers of Israel; Three Patriarchs; Two Tables of the Covenant; One God of the World.

Who knows Ten?

I know Ten: Ten Commandments; Nine Festivals; Eight Lights of Hanukkah; Seven Days of the Week; Six Days of Creation; Five Books of Moses; Four Mothers of Israel; Three Patriarchs; Two Tables of the Covenant; One God of the World.

Who knows Eleven?

I know Eleven: Eleven Stars in Joseph's Dream; Ten Commandments; Nine Festivals; Eight Lights of Hanukkah; Seven Days of the Week; Six Days of Creation; Five Books of Moses; Four Mothers of Israel; Three Patriarchs; Two Tables of the Covenant; One God of the World.

Who knows Twelve?

I know Twelve: Twelve Tribes; Eleven Stars; Ten Commandments; Nine Festivals; Eight Lights of Hanukkah; Seven Days of the Week; Six Days of Creation; Five Books of Moses; Four Mothers of Israel; Three Patriarchs; Two Tables of the Covenant; One God of the World.

Who knows Thirteen?

I know Thirteen: Thirteen Attributes of God*; Twelve Tribes; Eleven Stars; Ten Commandments; Nine Festivals; Eight Lights of Hanukkah; Seven Days of the Week; Six Days of Creation; Five Books of Moses; Four Mothers of Israel; Three Patriarchs; Two Tables of the Covenant; One God of the World.

* Exodus XXXIV: 6–7.

יְמֵי חֲנֻכָּה. שִׁבְעָה יְמֵי שַׁבְּתָא. שִׁשָּׁה סִדְרֵי מִשְׁנָה. חֲמִשָּׁה חֻמְשֵׁי תוֹרָה. אַרְבַּע אִמָּהוֹת. שְׁלֹשָׁה אָבוֹת. שְׁנֵי לֻחוֹת הַבְּרִית. אֶחָד אֱלֹהֵינוּ שֶׁבַּשָּׁמַיִם וּבָאָרֶץ:

עֲשָׂרָה מִי יוֹדֵעַ?

עֲשָׂרָה אֲנִי יוֹדֵעַ. עֲשָׂרָה דִּבְּרַיָּא. תִּשְׁעָה זְמַנֵּי שִׂמְחָה. שְׁמוֹנָה יְמֵי חֲנֻכָּה. שִׁבְעָה יְמֵי שַׁבְּתָא. שִׁשָּׁה סִדְרֵי מִשְׁנָה. חֲמִשָּׁה חֻמְשֵׁי תוֹרָה. אַרְבַּע אִמָּהוֹת. שְׁלֹשָׁה אָבוֹת. שְׁנֵי לֻחוֹת הַבְּרִית. אֶחָד אֱלֹהֵינוּ שֶׁבַּשָּׁמַיִם וּבָאָרֶץ:

אַחַד עָשָׂר מִי יוֹדֵעַ?

אַחַד עָשָׂר אֲנִי יוֹדֵעַ. אַחַד עָשָׂר כּוֹכְבַיָּא. עֲשָׂרָה דִּבְּרַיָּא. תִּשְׁעָה זְמַנֵּי שִׂמְחָה. שְׁמוֹנָה יְמֵי חֲנֻכָּה. שִׁבְעָה יְמֵי שַׁבְּתָא. שִׁשָּׁה סִדְרֵי מִשְׁנָה. חֲמִשָּׁה חֻמְשֵׁי תוֹרָה. אַרְבַּע אִמָּהוֹת. שְׁלֹשָׁה אָבוֹת. שְׁנֵי לֻחוֹת הַבְּרִית. אֶחָד אֱלֹהֵינוּ שֶׁבַּשָּׁמַיִם וּבָאָרֶץ:

שְׁנֵים עָשָׂר מִי יוֹדֵעַ?

שְׁנֵים עָשָׂר אֲנִי יוֹדֵעַ. שְׁנֵים עָשָׂר שִׁבְטַיָּא. אַחַד עָשָׂר כּוֹכְבַיָּא. עֲשָׂרָה דִּבְּרַיָּא. תִּשְׁעָה זְמַנֵּי שִׂמְחָה. שְׁמוֹנָה יְמֵי חֲנֻכָּה. שִׁבְעָה יְמֵי

שַׁבְּתָא. שִׁשָּׁה סִדְרֵי מִשְׁנָה. חֲמִשָּׁה חֻמְשֵׁי תוֹרָה. אַרְבַּע אִמָּהוֹת. שְׁלֹשָׁה אָבוֹת. שְׁנֵי לֻחוֹת הַבְּרִית. אֶחָד אֱלֹהֵינוּ שֶׁבַּשָּׁמַיִם וּבָאָרֶץ:

שְׁלֹשָׁה עָשָׂר מִי יוֹדֵעַ?

שְׁלֹשָׁה עָשָׂר אֲנִי יוֹדֵעַ. שְׁלֹשָׁה עָשָׂר מִדַּיָּא. שְׁנֵים עָשָׂר שִׁבְטַיָּא. אַחַד עָשָׂר כּוֹכְבַיָּא. עֲשָׂרָה דִבְּרַיָּא. תִּשְׁעָה זְמַנֵּי שִׂמְחָה. שְׁמוֹנָה יְמֵי חֲנֻכָּה. שִׁבְעָה יְמֵי שַׁבְּתָא. שִׁשָּׁה סִדְרֵי מִשְׁנָה. חֲמִשָּׁה חֻמְשֵׁי תוֹרָה. אַרְבַּע אִמָּהוֹת. שְׁלֹשָׁה אָבוֹת. שְׁנֵי לֻחוֹת הַבְּרִית. אֶחָד אֱלֹהֵינוּ שֶׁבַּשָּׁמַיִם וּבָאָרֶץ:

Ehod Mi Yodea

1. E - hod mi yo - de - a e - hod a - ni yo - de - a, *(Omit............)* e - hod elo - he - nu shebashsho - ma - yim u - vo - o - retz.
2. Sh' - na - yim mi yo - de - a, sh' - na - yim ani yo - de - a, sh' - ne lu - hos hab' - ris, e - hod elo - he - nu shebashsho - ma - yim u - vo - o - retz.

(Omit for first stanza)

Ḥad Gadyo

Allegorical meanings have been sought in the Ḥad Gadyo, on the supposition that it illustrates the working of Divine justice in the history of mankind. In reality, it is a rhyme for children, to keep their interest to the end of the Seder. As in the preceding number so in this one, grown people become children. The company reads in unison (not racing as in "Who Knows One" but) with regular rhythm, as to the beat of music; or sings it to one of the following musical settings.

An only kid!
An only kid,
My father bought
For two zuzim*.
An only kid! An only kid!

2. Then came the cat
And ate the kid
My father bought
For two zuzim.
An only kid! An only kid!

3. Then came the dog
And bit the cat
That ate the kid
My father bought
For two zuzim.
An only kid! An only kid!

* Pieces of money.

חַד גַּדְיָא חַד גַּדְיָא

דְּזַבַּן אַבָּא בִּתְרֵי זוּזֵי

חַד גַּדְיָא חַד גַּדְיָא:

וַאֲתָא שׁוּנְרָא

וְאָכַל לְגַדְיָא

דְּזַבַּן אַבָּא בִּתְרֵי זוּזֵי

חַד גַּדְיָא חַד גַּדְיָא:

וַאֲתָא כַלְבָּא.

וְנָשַׁךְ לְשׁוּנְרָא.

דְּאָכַל לְגַדְיָא.

דְּזַבַּן אַבָּא בִּתְרֵי זוּזֵי.

חַד גַּדְיָא חַד גַּדְיָא:

4. Then came the stick
   And beat the dog
   That bit the cat
   That ate the kid
   My father bought
   For two zuzim.
An only kid! An only kid!

5. Then came the fire
   And burned the stick
   That beat the dog
   That bit the cat
   That ate the kid
   My father bought
   For two zuzim.
An only kid! An only kid!

6. Then came the water
   And quenched the fire
   That burned the stick
   That beat the dog
   That bit the cat
   That ate the kid
   My father bought
   For two zuzim.
An only kid! An only kid!

וַאֲתָא חוּטְרָא.
וְהִכָּה לְכַלְבָּא.
דְּנָשַׁךְ לְשׁוּנְרָא.
דְּאָכַל לְגַדְיָא.
דְּזָבֵן אַבָּא בִּתְרֵי זוּזֵי.
חַד גַּדְיָא חַד גַּדְיָא:

וַאֲתָא נוּרָא.
וְשָׂרַף לְחוּטְרָא.
דְּהִכָּה לְכַלְבָּא.
דְּנָשַׁךְ לְשׁוּנְרָא.
דְּאָכַל לְגַדְיָא.
דְּזָבֵן אַבָּא בִּתְרֵי זוּזֵי.
חַד גַּדְיָא חַד גַּדְיָא:

וַאֲתָא מַיָּא.
וְכָבָה לְנוּרָא.
דְּשָׂרַף לְחוּטְרָא.
דְּהִכָּה לְכַלְבָּא.
דְּנָשַׁךְ לְשׁוּנְרָא.
דְּאָכַל לְגַדְיָא.
דְּזָבֵן אַבָּא בִּתְרֵי זוּזֵי.
חַד גַּדְיָא חַד גַּדְיָא:

7. Then came the ox
   And drank the water
   That quenched the fire
   That burned the stick
   That beat the dog
   That bit the cat
   That ate the kid
   My father bought
   For two zuzim.
An only kid! An only kid!

8. Then came the butcher
   And killed the ox
   That drank the water
   That quenched the fire
   That burned the stick
   That beat the dog
   That bit the cat
   That ate the kid
   My father bought
   For two zuzim.
An only kid! An only kid!

9 Then came the angel of death
   And slew the butcher
   That killed the ox

וַאֲתָא תוֹרָא.
וְשָׁתָא לְמַיָּא.
דְּכָבָה לְנוּרָא.
דְּשָׂרַף לְחוּטְרָא.
דְּהִכָּה לְכַלְבָּא.
דְּנָשַׁךְ לְשׁוּנְרָא.
דְּאָכַל לְגַדְיָא.
דְּזַבִּן אַבָּא בִּתְרֵי זוּזֵי.

חַד גַּדְיָא חַד גַּדְיָא: 
וַאֲתָא הַשּׁוֹחֵט.
וְשָׁחַט לְתוֹרָא.
דְּשָׁתָא לְמַיָּא.
דְּכָבָה לְנוּרָא.
דְּשָׂרַף לְחוּטְרָא.
דְּהִכָּה לְכַלְבָּא.
דְּנָשַׁךְ לְשׁוּנְרָא.
דְּאָכַל לְגַדְיָא.
דְּזַבִּן אַבָּא בִּתְרֵי זוּזֵי.

חַד גַּדְיָא חַד גַּדְיָא: 
וַאֲתָא מַלְאַךְ הַמָּוֶת.
וְשָׁחַט לְשׁוֹחֵט.
דְּשָׁחַט לְתוֹרָא.

That drank the water
That quenched the fire
That burned the stick
That beat the dog
That bit the cat
That ate the kid
My father bought
For two zuzim.
An only kid! An only kid!

10. Then came the Holy One, blest be He!
And destroyed the angel of death
That slew the butcher
That killed the ox
That drank the water
That quenched the fire
That burned the stick
That beat the dog
That bit the cat
That ate the kid
My father bought
For two zuzim.
An only kid! An only kid!

דְּשָׁתָא לְמַיָּא.
דְּכָבָה לְנוּרָא.
דְּשָׂרַף לְחוּטְרָא.
דְּהִכָּה לְכַלְבָּא.
דְּנָשַׁךְ לְשׁוּנְרָא.
דְּאָכַל לְגַדְיָא.
דְּזַבִן אַבָּא בִּתְרֵי זוּזֵי.

חַד גַּדְיָא חַד גַּדְיָא:

וַאֲתָא הַקָּדוֹשׁ בָּרוּךְ הוּא.
וְשָׁחַט לְמַלְאַךְ הַמָּוֶת.
דְּשָׁחַט לְשׁוֹחֵט.
דְּשָׁחַט לְתוֹרָא.
דְּשָׁתָא לְמַיָּא.
דְּכָבָה לְנוּרָא.
דְּשָׂרַף לְחוּטְרָא.
דְּהִכָּה לְכַלְבָּא.
דְּנָשַׁךְ לְשׁוּנְרָא.
דְּאָכַל לְגַדְיָא
דְּזַבִן אַבָּא בִּתְרֵי זוּזֵי.

חַד גַּדְיָא חַד גַּדְיָא:

Had Gadyo

Allegro moderato

Had gad - yo......... had gad - yo; di-z'-van ab-bo bis'-rè, zu - zé Had gad - yo......... had gad - yo.

va - so shun - ro, v' - o - chal l'-gad - yo, di-

z'-van ab-bo bis'- re zu - ze;

D.S. al 𝄌

va - so kal - bo v' - no - shach l'-shun -

ro, d' - o - chal l' - gad - yo, di -
z'-van ab-bo bis' - re zu - - ze.
D.S. al
va - so ḥut - ro v' - hik-koh l'-chal -

bo, d'-no-shach l'-shun - ro, d'-
o - chal l'-gad - yo, di - z'-van ab-bo
bis' - re zu - - ze.

D.S. al 𝄌

An Only Kid

Moderato

An on-ly kid, an on-ly kid.

1. An on-ly kid my fa-ther bought for two zu-zim.

2. Then came the cat and ate the kid, my fa-ther bought for

two zu-zim. 3. Then came the dog and bit the cat, that

ate the kid, my fa-ther bought for two zu-zim.

4. Then came the stick and beat the dog, that bit the cat, that

ate the kid, my fa-ther bought for two zu-zim.

5. Then came the fire and burned the stick, that beat the dog, that bit the cat, that ate the kid, my fa-ther bought for

two zu-zim. 6. Then came the water and quench'd the fire, that burned the stick, that beat the dog, that bit the cat, that ate the kid, my fa-ther bought for two zu-zim.

7. Then came the ox and drank the water, that quench'd the fire, that burned the stick, that beat the dog, that bit the cat, that ate the kid, my father bought for two zu-zim.

8. Then came the butcher and kill'd the ox, that drank the water, that quenched the fire, that burned the stick, that beat the dog, that bit the cat, that ate the kid, my father bought for

two zu-zim. **9.** Then came the angel of death and slew the butcher, that killed the ox, that drank the water, that quenched the fire, that burned the stick, that beat the dog, that

bit the cat, that ate the kid, my father bought for two zu-zim. 10. Then came the Holy One, blest be He! and destroyed the an-gel of death, that slew the butch-er, that killed the ox, that drank the water, that quenched the fire, that burned the stick, that beat the dog, that bit the cat, that ate the kid, my father bought for two zu-zim.

Vay'hi Bahatzi Hallay'loh

"AND IT CAME TO PASS AT MIDNIGHT."
All read the third line of each stanza in unison.

Unto God let praise be brought
For the wonders He hath wrought—
  At the solemn hour of midnight.

All the earth was sunk in night
When God said "Let there be light!"
  Thus the day was formed from midnight.

So was primal man redeemed
When the light of reason gleamed
  Through the darkness of the midnight.

To the Patriarch, God revealed
The true faith, so long concealed
  By the darkness of the midnight.

But this truth was long obscured
By the slavery endured
  In the black Egyptian midnight.

Till the messengers of light
Sent by God, dispelled the night,
  And it came to pass at midnight.

Then the people God had freed
Pledged themselves His law to heed,
   And it came to pass at midnight.

When they wandered from the path
Of the Lord, His righteous wrath
   Hurled them into darkest midnight.

But the prophets' burning word
By repentant sinners heard
   Called them back from darkest midnight.

God a second time decreed
That His people should be freed
   From the blackness of the midnight.

Songs of praise to God ascend,
Festive lights their glory lend
   To illuminate the midnight.

Soon the night of exile falls
And within the Ghetto walls
   Israel groans in dreary midnight.

Anxiously with God they plead,
Who still trust His help in need,
   In the darkest hour of midnight.

And He hears their piteous cry.
"Wait! be strong, My help is nigh,
   Soon 'twill pass — the long-drawn midnight.

"Tenderly I cherished you
For a service great and true;
   When 'tis past — the long-drawn midnight "

O, Thou Guardian of the Right,
Lead us onward to the light
   From the darkness of the midnight.

Father, let the day appear
When all men Thy name revere
   And Thy light dispels the midnight.

When no longer shall the foe
From th' oppressed wring cries of woe
   In the darkness of the midnight.

But Thy love all hearts shall sway;
And Thy light drive gloom away,
   And to midday change the midnight.

En Kelohenu

𝄋 f *Andante con moto*

1. En ke-lo-he-nu, En ka-do-ne-nu, En k'-mal-ke-nu, En k'mo-shi-e-nu. 2. Mi che-lo-he-nu, Mi cha-do-ne-nu,

3. No-de le-lo-he-nu, No-de la-do-,e-nu, No-de l'-mal-ke-nu, No-de l'mo-shi-e-nu. 4. Bo-ruch e-lo-he-nu, Bo-ruch a-do-ne-nu,

Mi ch'-mal ke nu Mi ch'moshi - e - nu.
Bo - ruch mal - ke - nu Bo - ruch moshi - e - nu.

5. At - to hu e - lo - he - nu, At to hu a - do - ne - nu, At - to hu mal - ke - nu, At - to hu mo - shi - e - nu.

America

1. My coun-try! 'tis of thee, Sweet land of lib-er-ty, Of thee I sing; Land where my fa-thers died! Land of the pilgrims' pride! From ev-'ry mountain side, Let freedom ring!

2. My na-tive coun-try, thee, Land of the no-ble free, Thy name I love; I love thy rocks and rills, Thy woods and templed hills: My heart with rapture thrills Like that a-bove.

3. Let music swell the breeze,
   And ring from all the trees
   Sweet freedom's song!
   Let mortal tongues awake;
   Let all that breathe partake;
   Let rocks their silence break,
   The sound prolong.

4. Our fathers' God, to Thee,
   Author of liberty,
   To Thee we sing:
   Long may our land be bright
   With freedom's holy light;
   Protect us by Thy might'
   Great God, our King!

RELIGIOUS LIBERTY

The Passover in History, Literature and Art.

THE PASSING GENERATIONS

History of the Passover

AS THE rocks of granite yield to the trained eye of the scientist the secret of their formation, so human institutions, properly examined, present records of growth. Such a story of development, in response to changing social conditions, is displayed by the feast of the Passover.

A. THE FESTIVAL OF THE SHEPHERDS.

Its name ḤAG HAPPESAḤ harks back to the misty dawn of history. Long before the Exodus, the pastoral tribes of Israel celebrated this festival of the shepherds. As among other pastoral tribes, so among our forefathers, the joyous springtime, with its rich manifestation of fertility through the offspring of the flocks and herds, called forth special festivities. Moses pleaded with Pharaoh in behalf of the Israelites: "Let us go, we pray thee, three days journey in the wilderness, and sacrifice unto the Lord our God; lest He fall upon us with pestilence, or with the sword". *
When they were refused, the Israelite families offered the Pesaḥ sacrifices in their homes in Egypt.

The exact meaning of the name given to this festival and the nature of its ceremonies are matters of conjecture. Its celebration in the early spring, was as-

* Exodus V: 3.

sociated with the sacrifice of the firstlings of the flocks and herds. The modified ordinance regarding its observance in Egypt, as given in Exodus XII, reads: "In the tenth day of this month they shall take to them every man a lamb, according to their fathers' houses, a lamb for a household; and if the household be too little for a lamb, then shall he and his neighbor next unto his house take one according to the number of the souls; according to every man's eating ye shall make your count for the lamb. Your lamb shall be without blemish, a male of the first year; ye shall take it from the sheep, or from the goats; and ye shall keep it until the fourteenth day of the same month; and the whole assembly of the congregation of Israel shall kill it at dusk. And they shall take of the blood, and put it on the two sideposts and on the lintel, upon the house wherein they shall eat it. And they shall eat the flesh in that night, roast with fire, and unleavened bread; with bitter herbs they shall eat it. Eat not of it raw, nor sodden at all with water, but roast with fire; its head with its legs and with the inwards thereof. And ye shall let nothing of it remain until the morning; but that which remaineth of it until the morning ye shall burn with fire. And thus shall ye eat it: with your loins girded, your shoes on your feet, and your staff in your hand; and ye shall eat it in haste — it is the Lord's passover."*

Only Israelites and initiated strangers could participate in the Passover. Through the partaking of the sacrificial meat, they sought to strengthen their union with one another and with God, and by means of consecrating their dwellings with the blood of the sacrifice, they hoped to ward off every harm and danger.

The departure of the Israelites from Egypt during

* Exodus XII: 3–11

the spring festival vested the ancient rite with new historical significance. The name Pesaḥ assumed the meaning of "passing over," of sparing and delivering, and its observance came to be interpreted as a memorial of God's appearance as the avenger of Israel's wrongs. The blood upon the doorposts and lintels was construed to have been a sign upon the homes of the Israelites to distinguish them from those of the Egyptians. Tradition described it as "the sacrifice of the Lord's passover, for that He passed over the houses of the children of Israel in Egypt, when He smote the Egyptians, and delivered our houses".*

B. THE FARMER'S SPRING FESTIVAL.

With their entrance into Canaan, the shepherd tribes of Israel began to follow agricultural pursuits. Among the older settlers of the land they found the custom of offering to the deity, at the spring of the year, the first fruit of their early harvest. They not only adopted this idea that an offering of their first grain was due to God, but extended it also to the firstlings of their flocks and herds. Thus the Passover sacrifice, while retaining its ancient ceremonials, received the new meaning of being a tribute due to God from the fold. It was also combined with the feast of Matzos or Unleavened Bread, the spring festival of the agricultural Canaanite community, observed in the month of Abib, before the beginning of the harvest season. The important feature of this celebration was the eating of matzos or cakes prepared of unleavened dough. As sacrificial food, it was to be free from leaven.**
"It is very probable", writes Dr. Julian Morgenstern, "that among the ancient Canaanites and the early

* Exodus XII: 27.
** Leviticus II: 11; VI: 10.

agricultural Israelites, the custom existed of destroying the usually meager remains of the old crop before the new crop could be used or even harvested. And if this hypothesis be correct, we must see in the ceremonies of the destruction of all leaven, of the fasting before the Matzos-festival and of the eating of the matzos themselves, the religious, sacramental rites by which the last remains of the old crop were destroyed as the necessary preparation for the cutting and eating of the new crop. All of the old crop was thus burned except just enough to prepare the matzos for the festival."*

The later law, as given in Leviticus XXIII:5ff, combines the pastoral and agricultural elements of the feast. It reads: "In the first month, on the fourteenth day of the month at dusk, is the Lord's passover. And on the fifteenth day of the same month is the feast of unleavened bread unto the Lord; seven days shall ye eat unleavened bread". On the second day of the feast, the barley harvest was ushered in by bringing a sheaf of the new crop unto the priest. "And he shall wave the sheaf before the Lord, to be accepted for you...And ye shall eat neither bread, nor parched corn, nor fresh ears, until this selfsame day, until ye have brought the offering of your God." From that day forty-nine days were counted, and the fiftieth was observed as Shabuoth (Feast of Weeks) or as Ḥag Habikkurim, the "feast of the first fruits". (In the orthodox synagogues the seven weeks between the first day of Pesaḥ and Shabuoth are still known as the season of S'firath Ho'omer, of "counting the sheaf".)

In the light of the association of the feast of Matzos with that of Pesaḥ, the eating of the matzos was re-interpreted as a reminder of the hurried flight of the

* The American Journal of Theology, vol. XXI, p. 288.

Israelites from Egypt. Exodus XII: 39 states: "And they baked unleavened cakes of the dough which they brought forth out of Egypt, for it was not leavened; because they were thrust out of Egypt, and could not tarry, neither had they prepared for themselves any victual".

C. THE FEAST OF ISRAEL'S BIRTH.

It was the tradition of the Exodus that vitalized the old Pesaḥ and Matzos festivals, and welded them into a distinctly Jewish institution, rich in ethical and religious possibilities. The national consciousness lovingly dwelt upon the fact that:

"When Israel came forth out of Egypt,

The house of Jacob from a people of strange language,

Judah became His sanctuary,

Israel His dominion."*

The hour which marked the birth of Israel as a holy nation, eloquently demonstrated to the religious mind the love of God for Israel. Prophetic idealism transformed this belief into a powerful lever of spiritual progress. "Ye have seen what I did unto the Egyptians", resounded the voice of God, "and how I bore you on eagles' wings, and brought you unto Myself. Now therefore, if ye will hearken unto My voice indeed and keep My covenant, then ye shall be Mine own treasure from among all peoples; for all the earth is Mine; and ye shall be unto Me a kingdom of priests, and a holy nation."** The belief in God's choice of Israel, determined Israel's mission in the world. The high privilege imposed great responsibility.

* Psalm CXIV: 1–2.
** Exodus XIX: 4–5.

As the people chosen by God, in accordance with His plan of the universal salvation of mankind, Israel must keep faith with God and be "a covenant of the people" and "a light of the nations:

> To open the blind eyes,
> To bring out the prisoners from the dungeon,
> And them that sit in darkness out of the prison-house".*

The conviction that Israel was delivered from its low estate to become the deliverer of the nations from moral and spiritual slavery, led to the comforting Divine assurance:

> "When thou passest through the waters, I will be with thee,
> And through the rivers, they shall not overflow thee;
> When thou walkest through the fire, thou shalt not be burned,
> Neither shall the flame kindle upon thee.
> For I am the Lord thy God,
> The Holy One of Israel, thy Savior;
> I have given Egypt as thy ransom,
> Ethiopia and Seba for thee.
> Since thou art precious in My sight, and honorable,
> And I have loved thee;
> Therefore will I give men for thee,
> And peoples for thy life.
> Fear not, for I am with thee."**

D. THE NATIONAL CELEBRATION.

(1) *The Passover During the Second Temple.*
As the feast of Israel's independence, the Passover

*Isaiah XLII: 6–7.
**Isaiah XLIII: 2–5.

steadily grew in the hearts of the people. It gained new power, when subsequent to the Deuteronomic reformation, under King Josiah (621 B.C.E.), the Passover sacrifices, like all other offerings, had to be brought to the national sanctuary at Jerusalem. During the entire period of the Second Temple the Passover celebration served as a strong influence in the unification of Israel. Josephus refers to the great alacrity with which the Jewish people celebrated the Passover, and states that on it "they are required to slay more sacrifices in number that at any other festival". He also points out that "an innumerable multitude came thither out of the country, nay, from beyond its limits also, in order to worship God". He estimates that one year, shortly before the fall of the Temple, the number of sacrifices reached 256,500, which, upon the allowance of ten to each sacrifice, together with the considerable number of foreigners and of Jews who were prevented from partaking of the Passover on account of bodily uncleanliness,* made the vast crowd that thronged the holy city upward of 2,700,200.

(2) *The Passover Sacrifice.***

For many days before the Passover, the people would come from every village and hamlet to celebrate the feast of unleavened bread in Jerusalem. By the fourteenth of Nisan the houses were crowded with guests, the open spaces were dotted with tents and the streets filled with the joyous pilgrims. Beneath the merrymaking, ran an undercurrent of earnest haste, for the great feast was close at hand. The houses were being

*Those that were prevented from performing their duty on the 14th of Nisan were allowed to offer the Passover sacrifice on the 14th of Iyar. See Numbers IX: 9-14.

**According to the Mishnah Pesaḥim.

cleaned of leaven, and special ovens were being prepared for the roasting of the paschal lambs.

Frequently in the midst of their labors, the people would look up to the Temple mount, where on one of the Temple galleries lay two sacrificial loaves, which served as a signal to them. As long as the priests allowed these loaves to remain, leavened bread could still be kept in the houses. But soon one loaf was removed, and then immediately afterwards the second loaf was taken away. At that signal fires leaped up all over the city. The last leaven was being burnt. For seven days thereafter only unleavened bread would be found in all the habitations of Israel.

Now the seventh hour of the day had passed and the regular daily offering had already been brought up. The time for the sacrifice of the paschal offering itself had come. Great throngs of people pressed against the gates of the Temple, each man leading his sacrificial lamb. Soon the gates were opened but only one-third of the throng was admitted. As they poured into the Temple courts, they beheld three rows of priests extending across the sacred precinct. The first and last rows carried silver basins, the intervening carried basins of gold. The first man carried his lamb to the altar where it was sacrificed. The blood was caught in one of the basins and handed from priest to priest, each one receiving the empty basin in return for the filled one. Thus with very little delay, all the sacrifices were completed. While these sacrifices were being performed, the Levites chanted aloud the Hallel Psalms, the people responding in unison. After the first group of pilgrims completed its sacrifices, the second group was admitted, and then the third. When all the sacrifices were over, the people went to their houses and proceeded to roast the paschal lamb and make all preparations for the great Seder service, which was to take place in every home that evening.

E. THE FEAST OF FREEDOM.

During the centuries of Roman oppression, when the Jewish people groaned under the crushing burden of the Caesars, even as did their forefathers in Egypt, the ancient Feast of Freedom was charged with new vitality. Its annual recurrence came like a summons to new life and to liberty, making each Israelite feel as if he personally had shared in the Exodus. This sentiment was fostered by the new ritual for the home which replaced the Passover sacrifice after the Temple and the altar had been destroyed. While the Seder service was commemorative of the sacrificial rites at the Temple (the roast bone representing the paschal lamb, and the egg the additional festive offerings, the Hagigah), it was essentially propagandist in nature. The recital of the story of the Exodus was calculated to awaken the national consciousness. It became a duty to tell the young and to rehearse to one another the tale of the deliverance from Egyptian bondage. To dwell at length on it was considered praiseworthy. During the Hadrianic persecution, we find Rabbi Akiba, the moving spirit in Bar Cochba's heroic struggle to regain the independence of the Jewish people, together with other leaders in Israel, at B'nai B'rak, absorbed in the story of the Exodus all night, looking to the fulfillment of the prophetic promise to Israel:

> As in the days of thy coming forth out of the land of Egypt
> Will I show unto him marvelous things.*

* Micah VII, 15.

Commemorating the deliverance from Egyptian bondage ("Pesaḥ Mitzrayim"), the Passover held out the promise of the future redemption from Roman bondage ("Pesaḥ L'osid"). Another belief, too, became current that God's anointed (the Messiah) would appear on the anniversary of Israel's liberation, to reestablish the fallen tabernacle of David. Several self-deluded men, under the spell of this belief, proclaimed themselves as the long expected Messiahs. Thus in all ages, the Passover proved to be a perennial source of hope. Celebrating it, the Jewish people defied their ever new Pharaohs and Caesars, declaring prayerfully: "This year we are slaves; next year may we be free men". To souls crushed with anguish the "Z'man Ḥerusenu—the season of our liberation" held out the promise of the coming day when all fetters of oppression would be broken, when the clouds of religious bigotry and racial prejudice and hatred would be dispelled by the dawning light of God's truth, and when Israel's dormant powers would awaken to new life and blossom forth in renewed glory.

THE ETHICAL SIGNIFICANCE OF THE PASSOVER.

Israel's experience was unique from the first when it departed from Egypt. Again and again races have been subjugated, reduced to slavery or villenage; but does history know of another horde of slaves that recovered itself, regained freedom, reestablished its own civilization, its own government? It is eminently proper, therefore, that in the prophetic as well as the Rabbinic cycle of ideas the Exodus from Egypt should occupy a prominent place. Its importance had been recognized still earlier, in the code, the Torah. The most exalted moral statutes concerning the treatment of strangers are connected with the Exodus, and are, from a psychologic point of view, impressively inculcated by means of the reminder: "Ye know the heart of the stranger!"* It is remarkable how even the law of the Sabbath rest, at first sight unconnected with the story of Israel's slavery and redemption, is brought into relation with and illuminated by it. The fourth commandment in the second version of the Ten Commandments, in Deuteronomy, disregards the dogmatic reason attached to the first ("for in six days the Lord made" etc).** It emphasizes the ethical motive, that the manservant and the maid-servant should be granted a day of rest, and employs the memory of the Egyptian experience to urge consideration for subordinates. This method, characteristic of the Bible and still more of the Rabbis, of establishing a connection between the most important moral laws and the history of Israel in Egypt, at the same time illustrates how nations should draw instruction from their fortunes.

The Prophets and Psalmists employ the great historical event to give reality chiefly to the religious idea of God's providence and grace. The Rabbis, finally, deduce from it the two fundamental elements of man's ethical educaton: the notion of liberty and the notion of man's ethical task.

Political and even civil freedom was lost. The Roman Pharaohs, if they did not exact labor, the more despotically exacted property and blood, and aimed at the annihilation of ideal possessions—the Law, its study, and its execution. Yet the notion of liberty, inner moral and spiritual liberty, cherished as a pure, exalted ideal, possible only under and through the Law, was associated with the memory of the redemption

* Exodus XXIII: 9.
** Exodus XX: 11.

from Egyptian slavery, and this memory in turn was connected with symbolic practices accompanying every act, pleasure, and celebration.

Moritz Lazarus,
The Ethics of Judaism, Part 1, p. 231-2 and 29.

MOSES AND THE TABLES OF THE LAW

Moses

"How small Sinai appears when Moses stands upon it! This mountain is only the pedestal for the feet of the man whose head reaches up to the heavens, where he speaks with God."

The artistic spirit was directed by Moses, "as by his Egyptian compatriots, to colossal and indestructible undertakings. He built human pyramids, carved human obelisks; he took a poor shepherd family and created a nation from it — a great eternal, holy people; a people of God, destined to outlive the centuries, and to serve as pattern to all other nations, even as a prototype to the whole of mankind. He created Israel," ... a people that has "fought and suffered on every battlefield of human thought."

Heinrich Heine

To lead into freedom a people long crushed by tyranny; to discipline and order such a mighty host; to harden them into fighting men, before whom warlike tribes quailed and walled cities went down; to repress discontent and jealousy and mutiny; to combat reactions and reversions; to turn the quick, fierce flame of enthusiasm to the service of a steady purpose, require some towering character — a character blending in highest expression the qualities of politician, patriot, philosopher, and statesman — the union of the wisdom of the Egyptians with the unselfish devotion of the meekest of men.

The striking differences between Egyptian and Hebrew polity are not of form but of essence. The tendency of the one is to subordination and oppression; of the other, to individual freedom. Strangest of recorded birth! From the strongest and most splendid despotism of antiquity comes the freest republic. From between the paws of the rock-hewn Sphinx rises the genius of human liberty, and the trumpets of the Exodus throb with the defiant proclamation of the rights of man... In the characteristics of the Mosaic institutions, as in the fragments of a Colossus, we may read the greatness of the mind whose impress they bear — of a mind in advance of its surroundings, in advance of its age; of one of those star souls that dwindle not with distance, but, glowing with the radiance of essential truth, hold their light while institutions and languages and creeds change and pass.

Leader and servant of men! Law-giver and benefactor! Toiler towards the Promised Land seen only by the eye of faith! Type of the high souls who in every age have given to earth its heroes and its martyrs, whose deeds are the precious possession of the race, whose memories are its sacred heritage! With whom among the founders of Empire shall we compare him?

To dispute about the inspiration of such a man were to dispute about words. From the depths of the Unseen such characters must draw their strength; from fountains that flow only for the pure in heart must come their wisdom. Of something more real than matter, of something higher than the stars, of a light that will endure when suns are dead and dark, of a purpose of which the physical universe is but a passing phase, such lives tell.

Henry George, Lecture on Moses, 1884

Preparations For The Passover

A. TIME OF THE FEAST.

Though the Bible calls for the observance of Passover for seven days, the changing conditions of Jewish life before the fall of Jerusalem (70 C.E.) produced an eighth day of the Feast. As the calendar was not yet established, the Sanhedrin, exercising its religious authority, proclaimed each New Moon ("Rosh Hodesh"), and thereby regulated the dates of the festivals. However, its decisions were not always conveyed to the distant Jewish settlements in time to celebrate the holy days at the right season. To obviate this difficulty, the Jewish communities, outside of Palestine, added an extra day to each festival. When a permanent calendar was finally framed by Hillel II, in 360 C.E., and the dates of the holy days were no longer in doubt, the Rabbis of Babylonia wished to drop the second day of festivals, but they were advised by the Palestinian authorities not to break an established custom. Reform Judaism, recognizing that this custom causes needless hardship to Jewish people, in commercial and industrial centers, abolished the second day of festivals. Accordingly reform Jews, following the biblical law, keep Passover seven days, beginning on the eve of the 15th and ending on the 21st of Nisan. The first and last days are holy days on which divine services are held in the synagogues. The intervening days, known as "Hol Hamoed" are half-holy days.

B. MATZO-BAKING.

With the cessation of the sacrificial cult the original distinction between the feast of Pesaḥ and that of Matzos disappeared to all practical purposes. The prominent feature of the feast came to be the eating of matzo. "The eating of matzo during Passover, unlike the prohibition against eating ḥometz, is not imperative; it is a voluntary act ('r'shus'). That is, a Jew may abstain from eating both ḥometz and matzo, except on the first eve, when the eating of matzo is obligatory ('ḥovoh')". Matzo may be made of flour of wheat, barley, spelt, oats, or rye. Special care must be exercised in kneading and baking to prevent the fermentation of the dough. "In the early centuries matzo-baking was done by the wife daily, for the household use. In the middle ages preparations were made to bake matzos thirty days before Passover, except the Matzo Sh'miroh ('observance Matzo', prepared with special care for use on the Passover eve by men of extreme piety), which was baked in the afternoon of the 14th of Nisan, at a time when the Passover lamb was formerly sacrificed. Still later, when the community had a communal oven, it was incumbent on the lord of the house to superintend the matzo-baking for his family.... About 1875 matzo-baking machinery was invented in England, and soon after introduced into America", where it became an important industry. To keep the matzo from rising and swelling in baking, it was perforated after being rolled into shape, by means of a 'reidel', or wheel provided with sharp teeth and attached to a handle. "The perforator, usually a youth, would run his reidel through the matzo in lines crossed at right angles and about one inch apart. The matzo-machine has an automatic perforator that makes lines at intervals of a half inch."*

C. REMOVING THE LEAVEN.

While the law regarding unleavened bread is simple, the prohibitions of the use of leaven, or ḥometz, during the Pesaḥ week, grew exceedingly complex. Rabbinical law forbids not only the eating of leavened bread but also the derivation of any benefit from it. Every trace of leaven has to be removed before the feast sets in. Hence there arose the quaint ceremony of "b'dikas ḥometz—searching for leaven", still observed by orthodox Jews. On the eve of the 14th of Nisan, i.e. on the night before Passover eve, after the evening service, the head of the house deposits crumbs of bread in conspicuous places, on window sills or open shelves, and, taking a wooden spoon in one hand and a few feathers in the other, begins the naive "search for leaven". The children enjoy the privilege of following him with a lighted taper. Blessing God for the command of removing the leaven, he proceeds, in strict silence, to sweep the crumbs into the wooden spoon with the feathers. When the task is done, he makes this solemn declaration, in Aramaic: "All manner of leaven that is in my possession, which I have not seen or removed, shall be as naught, and accounted as the dust of the earth". He then ties the spoon, feathers and leaven in one bundle and deposits it in a safe place. The following morning, after breakfast, he proceeds to burn the bundle of ḥometz. This ceremony, known as "bi'ur ḥometz—destruction of the leaven", is preceded by a declaration, similar to that

*J. D. Eisenstein art. "Mazza" in the Jewish Encyclopedia, vol. VIII, pp. 393–396.

made on the night before, disclaiming responsibility for any leaven that may still be found on the premises.

The Jewish mystics read a higher meaning into this as into all other ceremonies. Regarding hometz as the symbol of sordidness and corruption, they beheld in the ceremony of its removal a summons to man to destroy the evil of his heart.

D. "KASHERING" THE UTENSILS.

It is also customary among orthodox Jews to put away, for the period of the feast, all dishes and kitchen utensils that are used for the hometz, and to replace them with new ones or with such as are especially kept for Pesah. Some vessels are retained for the holiday after undergoing the process of "kashering", i.e. of being made fit for Passover use: glass-ware and porcelain are dipped into boiling water, and iron vessels are passed through fire and made hot.

Reform Judaism does not consider these practices essential to the proper observance of the Passover.

Survivals of The Ancient Passover

A. THE SAMARITAN PASSOVER.

The observance of the Passover by the Samaritan sect, native to Samaria, the central region of Palestine, casts much light upon this institution in biblical times. James A. Montgomery gives this interesting outline of the function:

"The solemnity is a veritable Haj, or pilgrim feast. The whole community proceeds to the place of sacrifice on Mount Gerizim, allowing abundance of time for the preparations. The tents are pitched, and all eagerly await the appointed hour, which occurs at sunset,—for so the Samaritans interpret the phrase 'between the evenings'.* A number of lambs have been carefully selected from those born in the preceding Tishri, and of these so many as will suffice for the worshippers are destined for the sacrifice, generally from five to seven, although others are at hand in case anyone of them is ritually unfit. Some hours before the sacrifice two fires are started in the trenches; in one of them a caldron is heated for boiling the water necessary to fleece the lambs, in the other a mass of fuel is kindled to make the oven for roasting the lambs. All these preparations are in the hands of young men,[**] who sometimes are clad in blue robes. Coincident with the starting of the fire, the service begins and

*Exodus XII: 6.
**Cf. Exodus XXIV: 5.

this is kept up until the lambs are put into the oven; it consists in the reading of the Passover lections from Exodus, and ancient Passover hymns. A certain number of representative men render the antiphons. In the service all turn toward the Kibla, the top of Gerizim. At sunset the sacrifice takes place, not on an altar but in a ditch; the throats of the lambs are deftly cut by a young man, not by the priest. The ritual inspection then takes place, the sinews of the legs are withdrawn,* the offal removed, and the lambs fleeced by aid of the hot water. The lambs are then spitted with a long stick run through their length, and are conveyed to the heated oven, over which they are laid, the spits protruding on either side, while above them is laid a thick covering of turf to seal the oven. The process of roasting takes three or four hours, during which time the worshipers may rest, the service being mostly intermitted. When it is deemed the proper time, the lambs are withdrawn, and present a blackened and repulsive aspect. A short service then ensues, the congregation now appearing with their loins girt up and their staves in their hands,** and when the service is over, veritably 'eat in haste', for they fall ravenously upon the coal-like pieces of flesh, devouring it and taking plattersful to the women and children, who remain in the tents. When all the flesh is consumed, the bones, scraps, wool, are carefully gathered up, and thrown into the still smoldering fire, until all is consumed, 'so that none of it remain till the morrow'. After the meal ablutions take place, and the ceremony is concluded with further prayers and chants. According to the prescriptions of Numbers IX, the 'Second Passover' is allowed.

*Genesis XXXII: 32.
**Exodus XII: 11.

"In close connection with the Passover is the feast of Unleaven, or Massot, which is reckoned as the second sacred feast, being distinguished from the Passover, although coincident with it, according to the language of the Law. On the 13th of the month a careful search is made for all leaven, which is scrupulously removed, and from the 14th day till the 21st no leaven may be eaten. The 21st is the great day of this feast, and on it they make pilgrimage to Gerizim, reading through the book of Deuteronomy on the way and at the village Makkada, where they finally halt."

The Samaritans, pp. 38–40.

B. THE PASSOVER AS OBSERVED BY THE FALASHAS.

The Jews of Abyssinia, known among their neighbors as Falashas, according to Dr. Jacques Faitlovitch, who has visited them and has pleaded their cause before the Jews of Europe and America, celebrate the Passover "for seven days, and during this time they eat only unleavened bread and do not drink any fermented drinks. Several days before the feast, the homes are carefully cleaned, all articles of clothing are properly washed, and all vessels and utensils thoroughly scoured and cleaned like new. Three days before Passover, they stop eating leavened bread and take nothing but dried peas and beans, and on the eve of Passover they abstain from all food until after the sacrifice of the paschal lamb. On this day, a little before the setting of the sun, all assemble in the court of the synagogue, and in the name of the entire community, the sacrificer offers the paschal lamb upon the altar. The ceremony is observed with great pomp; the ritual prescribed in the Bible for this sacrifice is followed punctiliously, and after the sacrifice is slaughtered and roasted, the meat is eaten with unleavened bread by the priestly assistants. It is in this manner that the festival is inaugurated. On the following days they assemble in the Mesgid ('the place of prayer') at fixed hours, observing a special ritual and reciting various prayers and biblical texts having reference to the Exodus of the Israelites from Egypt."

American Jewish Year Book, 5681. p. 89.

Passover and Christendom

A. PASSOVER AND EASTER.

The Jewish Passover, in modified form, became the leading festival of the Christian Church. The English name Easter "is derived from Eostre or Ostara, the Anglo-Saxon goddess of Spring, to whom the month answering to our April and called Eostre-monath, was dedicated. This month, Bede says, was the same as the *mensis paschalis* 'when the old festival was observed with the gladness of a new solemnity' ". In other European languages the name of the festival is derived through the medium of Latin and Greek from the Hebrew *pesaḥ*. The early Christians continued to observe the Jewish festivals, but invested them with new meanings. Thus the Passover, with the new conception added to it of Christ as the true Paschal Lamb and the first fruits from the dead, continued to be observed, and became the Christian Easter.* However, it is incorrect to speak of Pesaḥ as the Jewish Easter, for while Pesaḥ celebrates the deliverance of Israel from slavery, Easter commemorates the death and the legendary resurrection of the Christ.

The Seder, too, has exerted great influence upon Christianity. In his book on Jewish Contributions to Civilization, p.91, Joseph Jacobs writes: "The central

* See the article on Easter in the Encyclopedia Britannica, XIth edition, vol. VIII, pp. 828–829.

function of the Church service, the Mass, (or in Protestant Churches, the Communion), derives its 'elements' in the last resort, from the wine and unleavened bread used at the home service of the Passover; and Bickel (in "The Lord's Supper and the Passover Ritual") has shown that the original ritual of the Mass is derived from that of the Seder service."

B. PASSOVER AND PREJUDICE.

By a strange irony of fate the Passover season, the Spring-time of nature and of freedom, became the signal for the most furious attacks upon the Jews by their Christian neighbors. Unacquainted with Jewish customs and beliefs, many of them maintained an antagonistic and distrustful attitude toward the Jews. Any malicious superstition about Jewish rites found open ears among the ignorant rabble. Hence the care taken in preparing the matzos, and the use of red wine in the Seder service became fruitful sources of wild speculation. These things rendered the coming of the Passover a time of dread and anguish for the Jewish people.

C. BLOOD ACCUSATION.

The distinguished Frenchman, Anatole Leroy Beaulieu, writes feelingly about "that senseless charge which, for centuries, has cost the lives of so many Israelites in every country, although at no time has it been possible to fasten the slightest guilt upon a single Jew.

"In Russia, Poland, Roumania, Bohemia and Hungary, the common people believe that the Jews need Christian blood for the preparation of their unleavened bread, the Passover matzos. In the villages, even in the cities in Eastern Europe, where beneath a thin veneer of modern culture, so often are found the ideas and beliefs of the Middle Ages, the peasant and the laborer have no doubt that the Jews require the blood taken from Christian veins in order to celebrate their Passover. He does not know, this Magyar peasant or Russian moujik, that, according to the testimony of Tertullian and of Minucius Felix, the same absurd and odious charge was brought against the early Christians by the pagans, who, in their malicious thirst for damaging information, no doubt mistook for a real sacrifice the mystical immolation of the Lamb of the Eucharist. No sooner has a Christian child disappeared, no sooner have the police discovered the corpse of a young boy or girl in the river or in the town-moat, than the public voice accuses the knife of the 'schaechter', the Jewish butcher, even though the body may not bear a single mark of violence. This is so well known that murderers have been seen dragging the bodies of their victims through the alleys of the Jewish quarters, confident, thereby, to divert the suspicion and fury of the crowd."

> Israel among the Nations, pp. 36–7.
> See also Prof. H. L. Strack's article on Blood Accusation in the Jewish Encyclopedia, vol. II, pp. 260 ff.

D. CHRISTIAN PROTESTS.

Though we live in the bright sunlight of liberty, many of our brethren still dwell in lands of darkness and are still made victims of malice and hatred. The blood libel has been frequently employed against them by their enemies as a means of inciting the ignorant mobs to riots and pogroms. During the notorious Beilis trial, in 1912, the leading British authors, editors, scientists, statesmen and heads of all the Christian denominations issued the following statement:

"We desire to associate ourselves with the protests signed in Russia, France, and Germany by leading Christian Theologians, Men of Letters, Scientists, Politicians, and others against the attempt made in the City of Kieff to revive the hideous charge of Ritual Murder — known as the 'Blood accusation' — against Judaism and the Jewish people.

"The question is one of humanity, civilization, and truth. The 'blood accusation' is a relic of the days of witchcraft and 'black magic', a cruel and utterly baseless libel on Judaism, an insult to the Western culture, and a dishonor to the Churches in whose name it has been falsely formulated by ignorant fanatics. Religious minorities other than the Jews, such as the early Christians, the Quakers, and Christian Missionaries in China, have been victimized by it. It has been denounced by the best men of all ages and creeds. The Popes, the founders of the Reformation, the Khaliff of Islam, statesmen of every country, together with all the great seats of learning in Europe, have publicly repudiated it."

Reform Judaism and Passover

One thing to me is clear: namely, the urgent present duty of all Liberal Jews to observe the Passover. And when I say "to observe" it, I mean to observe it properly with its ancient symbolism and its ancient forms. This means that Liberal Jews must (a) observe the first and seventh day of Passover as days of "rest" and worship; (b) observe the old ceremonial whereby for seven days unleavened bread is eaten at meals. It is also eminently desirable to retain in some modified form the domestic service upon the first night of the festival... The Passover celebrates the beginning of the self-consciousness of Israel; the setting forth of Israel upon its mission...It is the festival which commemorates the giving of a charge, the founding of a mission, the institution of a brotherhood, which were intended to spread the knowledge of God throughout the world.

Again, the Passover is the festival of liberty — liberty in political life, liberty in moral life, liberty in religious life. How immense the range!

But what is Liberty? It is freedom through law. Passover leads on to Pentecost, the festival which celebrates the giving of the Law.

Claude Montefiore, Outlines of Liberal Judaism, p. 254–6.

ISRAEL'S JOURNEY.

Long must be thy journey, O Israel, jubilee-crowned, long must it still continue! But wearied, wearied thou wilt never be! Still in thy native strength dost thou stand, O incomparable one! Still does the youthful blood flow lustily in thy veins! Still awaitest thou with the glowing ardor of battle, the countless hosts thou wilt in the end marshal for thy God. Nor, having marked the path which thou hast trod, can we ever doubt thy signal victory at last. Rejoice, then, in thy natal feast, O Israel, and take from us anew our solemn vows to cling unto thee with undying love and faith for ever!

David Einhorn, Sinai, vol. 1.

FREEDOM.

The high aim sanctified by time and by Judaism is, that all men be free, all recognize God, all employ their spiritual and material powers with full and free desire, so that a throne be built for truth and justice on this earth, a throne which shall adorn the lowliest hut as well as the most glorious palace.

Samuel Hirsch, The Reform Movement in Judaism, by David Philipson, p. 487.

Freedom is the indispensable condition of goodness' virtue, purity and holiness...Take away freedom from human nature and whatever remains of it is an anomaly, some nameless thing of human form and animal indifference. "Wisdom and cognition", of which the prophet speaks as "the stability of thy times and the fort of thy salvation", are the golden fruits of the free reason, the free-willed man only; they ripen not in the dark and dismal dungeon of the enslaved soul.

Isaac Mayer Wise, Sermons by American Rabbis, 1896, p. 181.

THE SEASON OF JOY.

However burdensome the Passover minutiae, especially in regard to the prohibition of leaven, became to the Jewish houshold, the predominant feature was always an exuberance of joy. In the darkest days of medievalism the synagogue and home resounded with song and thanksgiving, and the young imbibed the joy and comfort of their elders through the beautiful symbols of the feast and the richly adorned tale of the deliverance (the Haggadah). The Passover feast with its "night of divine watching" endowed the Jew ever anew with endurance during the dark night of medieval tyranny, and with faith in "the Keeper of Israel who slumbereth not nor sleepeth". Moreover, as the springtide of nature fills each creature with joy and hope, so Israel's feast of redemption promises the great day of liberty to those who still chafe under the yoke of oppression. The modern Jew is beginning to see in the reawakening of his religious and social life in western lands the token of the future liberation of all mankind. The Passover feast brings him the clear and hopeful message of freedom for humanity from all bondage of body and of spirit.

Kaufman Kohler, Jewish Theology, p. 462.

THE SECRET OF THE FEAST.

The great redemption holds us with its fascination, but only to bid our hearts go out to all the history of our race. This people "saved of the Lord with an everlasting salvation"—this people that gave the world Moses and the Prophets and the Saints, that has lived and died for God's truth—this people, we say, is ours. We are the sharers of its glories and its humiliations, the heirs to its divine promise and its sublime ideals. This people, we say moreover, began its life with a protest against wrong. It has lived its life protesting against wrong. And it has done so by moral force alone. Inherently weak, it has been made mighty by its cause, so that "no weapon formed against it has prospered" —neither persecution nor calumny, neither the sword nor the stake, neither the world's enticements nor the persuasive arts of an alien priesthood. Powerful nations have tried to destroy it; but they have perished, while their would-be victim has lived on. We who seemed "appointed to die" are the living history of the dead nations; for their annals are written with pen of iron upon the sacred soul of our race. 'This", we cry, "is the finger of God". A people is not thus wondrously preserved to live aimlessly. Still is God's mighty arm outstretched. "As in the days of our coming forth out of the land of Egypt God will show us marvelous things".

Morris Joseph, The Message of Judaism, pp.101-2.

The Haggadah

A. THE GROWTH OF ITS LITERATURE.

THE Haggadah, like the feast which it celebrates, is the slow growth of centuries, re-echoing battle-cries of Israel's heroic struggle for life and for freedom. Its oldest stratum consists of the Hallel* wherein triumphal songs, celebrating the deliverance from Egypt, mingle with supplications for Israel's future well-being. These were intoned, at the Temple of Jerusalem, by the Levitical choirs, during the preparation of the paschal sacrifices and were subsequently sung at the table after the festive family meal. Of high antiquity, too, are the blessings over the wine, the Kiddush, the four questions and their answers, based on Deuteronomy XXVI: 5-9. During the century that followed the destruction of the Temple (in the year 70 C.E.), important additions were made to the Haggadah, including the homily of Rabban Gamaliel, the composite prayer of Rabbi Tarfon and Rabbi Akiba asking for the reestablishment of the sacrificial service, the complete grace after the meal and the Birkas Hashir.**

---

* Psalm CXIII–CXVIII and CXXXVI.
**Taken to be the Yehalelucho or the Nishmas. See Pesaḥim X.

As the struggle against the Roman Pharaohs grew in intensity, the Jewish people welcomed into the Haggadah the mathematical disquisitions of the Rabbis Jose the Gallilean, Eliezer and Akiba regarding the number of plagues that were visited upon Egypt. As a protest against their revilers and tormentors, they also embodied into the Pesaḥ ritual the biblical imprecations against the heathens that know not God and devour Jacob and lay waste his habitation.*

The character of the Haggadah was further affected by the theological ideas which Judaism was called upon to combat. An echo of its conflict with early Christianity is found in the strong emphasis laid in the Haggadah on the fact that Israel's deliverance was effected by God in person, without the aid of intermediaries. The further struggle of Judaism against Karaism left a marked impress upon the very structure of the book. On the theory that he who dwells at length on the story of the Passover is praiseworthy, it became customary to include in the Haggadah, passages from the early Midrashic and the Talmudic writings, dealing with the Exodus. In the eighth century, when the Karaitic sect, in its opposition to Rabbinism, excluded these and other passages from the ritual, the masters of the Babylonian academies (the Geonim) took steps to standardize the homiletical sections of the Haggadah. While

*Psalm LXXIX: 6–7; LXIX: 26 and Lamentations III: 66.

the service retained its elasticity for several more generations (as evidenced from Saadia Gaon's and Maimonides' Haggadahs*) the text as drawn up by Rav Amram (about 850 C.E.)was adopted by Spanish Jewry and became the standard for all Israel.

The subsequent additions to the Haggadah consist of its poetic numbers. When the Haggadah began to circulate in separate book form (in the 13th century), it was enriched by Joseph Tov Elem's poem "Ḥasal Siddur Pesaḥ" (The Order of the Pesaḥ Service is Complete), Jannai's "Vay'hi Ba-ḥatzi Hallay'lo" (And it Came to Pass at Midnight), and Eliezer Ha-Kalir's "Va-Amartem Zevaḥ Pesaḥ" (And Ye Shall Say: This is the Passover Sacrifice), compositions originally written for other purposes. In the fifteenth century the two anonymous ditties "Addir Hu" and "Ki Lo Noeh" were added. About the same time the folk-songs "Eḥod Mi Yodea"and "Ḥad Gadyo" became part of the service, largely under German influence. The Sephardim have refused to admit them into their ritual. The cumulative effect of the varied literature of the Haggadah, of "the curious medley of legends and songs"and prayers, captivated the hearts of many generations of our people and filled them with a sense of special privilege of being part of Israel, the champion of God and of liberty.

B. REFORM JUDAISM AND THE HAGGADAH.

It was but natural for reform Judaism, which found itself at variance with a number of passages in the Haggadah, to construct a ritual for Pesaḥ eve in keeping with its religious principles. Among the German attempts, in this direction, are Leopold Stein's ritual (1841), David Einhorn's (in his Gebetbuch "Olas Tomid",1858) and S. Maybaum's(1893). An English Hag-

* See A. L. Frumkin's Siddur Rav Amram, p. 213 ff, and Mishneh Torah, Z'manim, Appendix to Hilchos Ḥometz u-Matzo.

gadah by H.M. Bien, misnamed "Easter Eve", appeared in 1886. The first edition of the Union Prayerbook (1892) contained a ritual for the Seder, based on Leopold Stein's German work. After its elimination from the subsequent editions of the Union Prayerbook, it was published by its author, I. S. Moses, in separate book form. In 1908, the Central Conference of American Rabbis issued the Union Haggadah. The work was executed in a modern spirit, no longer regarding "rites and symbols with the awe that vested them with mystic meaning, or supernatural sanction", but treating them rather as "potent object-lessons of great events and of sublime principles hallowed and intensified in meaning by ages of devout usage". Among the poetic additions to the Haggadah were Leopold Stein's "The Festive Cup" and Jannai's poem "Vay'hi Ba-ḥatzi Hallay'lo" both translated by Rabbi Henry Berkowitz, and Rabbi G. Gottheil's hymn "God of Might." The volume also contained the familiar Passover music, as edited by the Society of American Cantors, and the setting for "The Festive Cup", composed by the Rev. William Lowenberg.

The aim of the present edition of the Union Haggadah is stated in the introduction. The Committee on Revision reedited both the Hebrew and the English texts of the Union Haggadah and added the following musical numbers: "The Springtide of the Year" by Alice Lucas with the traditional music, as published in the Union Hymnal; "To Thee Above" by James K. Gutheim, with music specially written for it by Hugo Brandt; the traditional "Kiddush" melody with an accompaniment supplied by Rabbi Jacob Singer; traditional settings for Psalms CXIII and CXIV, arranged by D. M. Davis, and the Sephardic Hallel (Psalm CXVII) from F. L. Cohen's "Voice of Prayer and Praise"; a variation of the "Addir Hu" melody for Psalm CXVIII: 1–4; F. Halevy's settings for the responses "Zeh Hayyom" and "Hodu Ladonoi"; and S. Naumbourg's "Ono Adonoi"; also Alois Kaiser's music for "An Only Kid", from Rabbi William Rosenau's "Seder Haggadah"; and "America'. In addition the committee prepared a new Appendix. With the original Committee the present Committee on Revision may lay claim to having been guided by "reverent devotion to the sanctifying force of tradition and a due recognition of its supreme value as a bond of union", in its endeavor to present for men and women of to-day a Haggadah, modern in spirit and social outlook.

C. ILLUMINATED HAGGADAHS.

As the principal ritual work for the home, the Haggadah has enjoyed great popularity. Hundreds of learned scholars delighted to comment on its content, and innumerable scribes to copy and illuminate its text. Since the introduction of printing, the Haggadah has appeared in more than a thousand editions. Of the twenty-five known illuminated manuscript Haggadahs, the Sarajevo manuscript deserves special mention.* Israel Abrahams writes** that "the Sarajevo book must remain supreme as an introduction to Jewish art, so long as it continues to be the only completely reproduced Hebrew illuminated manuscript of the Middle Ages." The still unpublished Crawford Haggadah (now in the Rylands Library, Manchester) rivals the Sarajevo manuscript in point of age and of artistic excellence. "The beauty of the Crawford Haggadah consists just in the text, in the beautiful

* It was published by Mueller and Von Schlossar, 1898, and by Stassof and Guenzberg, 1905.

** By-Paths in Hebraic Bookland, pp. 91–96.

margins, full of spirited grotesques and arabesques, no doubt (like the Sarajevo manuscript itself) produced in Spain under strong North French influence."* In the Sarajevo Haggadah "we have, in the full page drawings, depicted the history of Israel from the days of the Creation, the patriarchal story, Joseph in Egypt, the coming of Moses, the Egyptian plagues, the Exodus, the revelation, the temple that is yet to be."... It is noteworthy that in the revelation picture no attempt is made to depict the Deity. "Into Moses' ear a horn conveys the inspired message; but the artist does not introduce God. ... Certainly the drawings, sadly though they lack proportion, are realistic. Especially is this true of the portrayal of Lot's wife transformed into a pillar of salt. Disproportionate in size, for she is taller than Sodom's loftiest pinnacles, yet the artist has succeeded in suggesting the gradual stiffening of her figure: we *see* her becoming rigid before our eyes."

Rachel Vishnitzer points out the French Gothic style in the illustrations of the "Two Medieval Haggadahs" of the British Museum.** The one with the fleur-de-lis*** exhibits a rich store of fanciful decorated forms. "There are lions, dogs, peacocks, salamanders, serpents, herons, griffins, hares and so on. Acorns, pomegranates and acanthus-leaves appear with the Gothic ivy-leaf as the prominent floral ornaments; then we can admire on the margins of the fine vellum sheets amusing fights between beasts, hare-hunting, little domestic scenes, caricatures of monks and various grotesque subjects agreeable to the taste of the time, executed with delightful finesse of design and coloring. It is very in-

* Mueller and Von Schlossar describe twenty other extant illustrated manuscripts in their above-named book.

**The Jewish Guardian, April 22, 1921.

***Brit. Mus. Add. 14,761.

teresting, moreover, to observe the skillful master of this unparalleled decoration, when he paints the human form and to see how helpless he becomes then."

"The second Haggadah* is quite different in conception and in the execution of the paintings. We recognize there an honest attempt at faithfully representing nature and of graphic interpretation of scenes from Bible history. The paintings are in keeping with the text of Exodus. Moses at the burning bush, his miracles, the plagues of Egypt, the Exodus from Egypt by the Israelites — all the stages of the story — are minutely depicted."

One of the Haggadahs in the Germanic museum at Nuremberg is especially noteworthy for illustrations of domestic scenes relating to the Seder service. "The fifteenth century Haggadah in the Bibliotheque Nationale has initials and domestic and historic scenes; while an elaborate manuscript in the possession of Baron Edmond de Rothschild has highly original domestic and biblical scenes executed in quatrocento style."**

Since the introduction of printing, about two hundred illustrated editions of the Haggadah have made their appearance. Their styles are for the most part determined by the Prague edition of 1526, of the Mantua edition of 1560, and of the Venice edition of 1599. Though they display a "distinct tendency toward monotony", some of them are not without charm.

The first edition of the Union Haggadah sought "an artistic expression for the Passover sentiment which shall reflect the present era". To this end it reproduced Moritz D. Oppenheim's "Seder Eve", the picture

* Or. 1,404 Brit. Mus., exhibiting much similarity with Lord Crawford's manuscript.

** Joseph Jacobs, Jewish Encyclopedia, Vol. VI, p. 144.

of Moses Ezekiel's statue "Religious Liberty" and the "Seder Dish" from Rosenau's "Jewish Ceremonial Institutions". It was also provided with pen-and-ink decorations and with pictures of two reliefs by Miss Katherine M. Cohen. The present edition has retained the three first-mentioned pictures, and has added G. Doré's "The Exodus" and the masterly relief of Moses and the Table of the Law, from an Italian Synagogue, dated 1671, reproduced in the Jewish Encyclopedia, vol. XI, p.663. The book has been further enriched by the decorative frontispiece, borders' and lettering specially prepared for it by Mr. Isadore Lipton. He has utilized authentic material from the Egyptian monuments and from ancient Jewish life, for the purpose of making real to our generation the ever fresh story of our deliverance. In his way, he sought to accomplish for the twentieth century what the unknown illustrators of the Sarajevo, the Crawford, the Prague and the Mantua Haggadahs accomplished for their times.